The Collector's Guide to

# HALL CHINA

## Margaret & Kenn Whitmyer

**COLLECTOR BOOKS**
*A Division of Schroeder Publishing Co., Inc.*

The current values in this book should be used only as a guide. They are not intended to set prices, which vary from one section of the country to another. Auction prices as well as dealer prices vary greatly and are affected by condition as well as demand. Neither the Author nor the Publisher assumes responsibility for any losses that might be incurred as a result of consulting this guide.

# Dedication

This book is dedicated to Dan Tucker and Lorrie Kitchen who have the fatal "Hall China Collection Syndrome." Harmless to humans, but deadly for the pocketbook; the collecting is fun. They invite you to join them.

# Contents

### PART V: OTHER HALL PRODUCTS

# Acknowledgements

This book was made possible through the gracious generosity of Hall China enthusiasts throughout the country. Veteran collectors happily loaned their cherished treasures and donated their time to enable us to reproduce as accurate an account as possible on the subject of Hall China. We appreciate their help and sincerely hope they are not disappointed with the result.

Dealer-collectors Dan Tucker and Lorrie Kitchen were instrumental in locating and providing us with material to photograph. Dan also had the ability to find those rare pieces when we needed them. Also the undying support and encouragement of these two friends eliminated many seemingly insurmountable obstacles.

The help of Everson Hall, current historian of the Hall China Company, is deeply appreciated. He donated his time to provide us with an insight into the history and production of Hall china. Interesting tours are available at the East Liverpool plant and the outlet store--The Hall Closet--provides an interesting selection of items currently available at reasonable prices.

We are also very grateful to the following people who loaned us parts of their collections to photograph or supplied us with needed information: Ken and Carol Baker, Joyce and Parke Bloyer, Don and Irma Brewer, Bob Brushaber, Sam and Becky Collings, Jim and Betty Cooper, Krystol Ellis, Gene Florence, Leonard and Shirley Graff, Woody Griffith, Joyce Guilmire, Art Hansen, Sonny and Betty Harris, Jerry Harris, Mr. & Mrs. Joseph Lockard, Merle and Dee Long, Robert and Bernadette Ludwig, Nancy Maben, Jerry and Connie Monarch, Benjamen Moulton, Tom and Jean Niner, Willie Price, Millie Smith, Sue Switzer, Lee Wagner, and Delmer and Mary Lou Youngen.

Again the efforts of our fine photographer, Siegfried Kurz, produced excellent results. We appreciate his patience in withstanding almost a full year of monthly photo sessions.

# Foreword

The purpose of this book is to provide collectors with a general guide to the most popularly collected pieces of Hall China. Currently the period of greatest collector interest in the products of the Hall China Company lies between the early 1930's and the early 1950's. We have tried to illustrate and identify as many pieces from this period as possible. However, new pieces are being discovered every day. Some other pieces in certain patterns should exist, but we have not included items in the listing which have not been confirmed.

Most of Hall's institutional line and patterns later than the fifties have not been included since there is still not much collector interest in these items. Some people are currently buying some of the institutional pieces to use in their kitchens, but these pieces have little collectible value.

Metal items and other accessory pieces which match Hall patterns, but were not produced by Hall, are also included in this guide. Many collectors are now incorporating these items into their collections.

Many of the names, patterns, and colors used in this book are Hall's. However, Hall did not have names for everything they made. In the event an official Hall name was not designated, we have taken the liberty of providing one of our own. The new names we have used will be found in quotation marks.

# Pricing

The prices in this book represent retail prices for mint condition pieces. A price range has been included to help account for regional differences in prices. Also be aware that certain rare pieces which are currently valued at several hundred dollars may prove to be hard-to-sell if a number of these items are discovered. Some items, which to date are one-of-a-kind may not be priced if a retail value has not been established.

Pricing information has been obtained from dealer listings, flea market and show observations, trade publications, and from collectors. Remember prices in this guide should be used only as a reference. Prices may vary in the marketplace and it is not the intention of the authors to establish or control prices.

# History of the Hall China Company

The Hall China Company was established by Robert Hall in 1903. The first plant was located at Fourth and Walnut Streets in East Liverpool, Ohio. Initially, three kilns and thirty-eight potters produced combinets and spittons. Robert Hall died the next year and his son, Robert Taggert Hall became manager.

Robert T. Hall experimented endlessly to rediscover a lost process from the Ming Dynasty (A.D. 1368-1644). in China, which would allow him to produce china by a single-fire process. This single-firing would allow the glaze to penetrate the unfired body, creating a craze-proof finish.

The leaded glazes of the period were not suitable to a process of this type, since they could not withstand the higher temperatures needed to fire the clay in a one-step process. Robert Taggert Hall experimented from 1903 to 1911, before he successfully produced the first leadless-glazed china using the single-fire process at a temperature of 2400°F. This new process produced colorfully-glazed china which was strong, non-porous, and crazeproof.

As the company grew, and the institutional line expanded, two more plants were added in East Liverpool. Finally, in 1930, all the separate operations were combined in a single plant on the east side of East Liverpool, where the Hall China Company still operates today. This production is again targeted primarily at institutional and commercial customers. However, Hall China still is mostly a hand operation and is able to easily adjust its schedule to accomodate various special order customers.

## The China Process

The manufacture of Hall china begins with a secret powdered mixture of flint, feldspar, and several different clays. These ingredients are mixed with water in a machine. The resulting slip is passed through separators which remove metals and other foreign objects.

The mixture is then pumped into presses which squeeze out the water, leaving clay in a cake form. The cakes of clay are then aged and pressed through pug mills which remove the air from the clay.

The clay is then shaped by a "jiggerman" on a potters' wheel to form flat pieces or bowls. To produce pieces such as teapots or jugs, water is added to the clay, and the resulting slip is poured in a mould. The raw ware is allowed to dry for twenty-four hours at about 100°F. Then the special leadless glaze is applied by either spraying or hand-dipping. The glazed pieces are placed on cars which move slowly through a tunnel kiln. The temperature of the ware slowly increases to 2400°F. This intense heat causes chemical changes in the body and the glaze materials which cause the color to set.

The fired china is then inspected for defects and the good pieces are sent on to the decorating department. Decorating is done either by hand painting or by transferring decals or prints to the ware. The finished product is then refired in a smaller oven at a lower temperature. Decals were a very popular method of decoration during the thirties and forties. Since only pieces of large decals were sometimes used on smaller pieces in a pattern, it is sometimes difficult to associate these pieces with the rest of the items in a pattern. Careful comparison will usually result in a positive identification.

# Identification of Hall China

#1    #2    #3    #4    #5

Mark #1 is a very early mark. This mark is only found on early institutional ware and will not be found on "collectible" Hall. The mark was probably used from sometime after the beginning and into the early teens.

Mark #2 can be dated from the early teens into the late twenties. This mark will not be found on much "collectible" Hall except a few very early teapots.

Mark #3 is the mark which appears most frequently on items of interest to today's collectors. This mark was used from the early thirties to the early seventies and will be found on most items except kitchenware and dinnerware. These two items received special marks.

Mark # 4, the "HALL SUPERIOR QUALITY KITCHENWARE" mark, was used on all kitchenware made after 1932. This mark was usually stamped in gold, but may also be found in black.

Mark #5 was reserved for Hall dinnerware. This mark was modified slightly for use with dinnerware of the Jewel Tea Company and for the Orange Poppy and Wildfire lines of the Great American Tea Company. Autumn Leaf will have "Tested and Approved by MARY DUNBAR--JEWEL HOMEMAKERS INSTITUTE" in the circle. Orange Poppy has the Great American Golden Key symbol inside the circle and the Wildfire mark honors the celebration of the 100th anniversary of Great American.

Hall China was proud to mark most of the pieces they produced. This makes the job of identifying Hall China easier for collectors. Most pieces of Hall which were not marked, except for shakers, were seconds and never reached the decorating room.

In addition to the printed stamps, some pieces, especially the early institutional ware was embossed with "HALL" in large block letters.

Paper labels were also used by Hall. However, since most of the pieces were used heavily, not much Hall china is found with the paper labels still intact. We have seen a few items in which the paper label has been helpful in identification. One example is the lamp pictured on page 158. This lamp has an Aladdin teapot-shaped paper label and is the only means by which the lamp can be attributed to Hall.

Hall china produced since the early 1970's has the following mark:

# Colors

Hall produced the widest variety of colored glazes of any china company. Many of the colors are very close, with some only varying by a shade. Due to this small difference we have tried to reproduce some of the most frequently encountered colors in the accompanying color chart. Even with the help of the chart it may still be hard to identify some of the colors.

| Ivory | Hi-white | Addison | Cobalt | Blue Turquoise | Turk Blue |
| Cadet | Delphinium | Dresden | Marine | Sandust | Tan |
| Stock Brown | Mahogany | Stock Green | Forest Green | Turquoise | Green Lustre |
| Emerald | Garden | Monterrey | Lettuce | Celadon | Seaspray |
| Old Rose | Rose | Pink | Sunset | Poppy | Indian Red |
| Camellia | Maroon | Chinese Red | Daffodil | Canary | Warm Yellow |

*"I am courteous, dependable, prompt—and a loyal American"*

## Dear Mrs. Brown
### —WE'RE BOTH LUCKY
### IF YOU LIVE IN ONE OF
### THE COMMUNITIES I SERVE

**"HERE'S WHY:** My company—the Jewel Tea Company—delivers fresh coffees, teas, groceries and laundry products, direct to your home. We share with you the savings of this direct method of selling, by giving you attractive premiums.

**"HERE'S HOW IT WORKS:** With every dollar's worth of groceries you buy, you receive generous profit-sharing credits toward some useful household article—a coffee maker, electric clock, a pair of blankets, rug, set of silverware, cooking utensil, set of dishes, etc. And I bring the premium to you *right away*, so you can enjoy it while you are using the groceries.

**"HERE'S HOW MUCH YOU SAVE:** I bring you, on an average, $1.20 worth of coffee, groceries and useful household articles, for each $1.00 you spend with me. Think how 20c *more* for your grocery dollar would help out your household budget!

**"HERE'S SMART SHOPPING:** It is *smart* and *time-saving* to shop the Jewel way—to do the ordering right in your home, to have deliveries made right to your kitchen table, and to receive all sorts of attractive, useful premiums—*without any extra cost*. My company is an old, established firm—started in 1899—and now serving more than a million homes. My spotless coffee-brown and cream Jewel car is recognized everywhere as a symbol of thrifty, convenient grocery buying.

**"HERE'S GOOD NEWS:** This year, new thousands of homes will benefit from my company's expansion program. Already the women of 43 states and 16,000 communities enjoy Jewel service. Each week it is being extended to *two more communities*. If yours is one of them, I'll welcome the chance to tell you about the Jewel Way of getting useful premiums with your coffee and groceries without extra cost. Look up Jewel Tea Co., Inc. in your phone book or write to my company."

*Chicagoans are lucky, too! Clean, white, super Jewel Food Stores are the fastest growing group in Chicagoland. Headquarters for the best in meats, groceries, and fresh fruits and vegetables.*

## The Jewel Man

**JEWEL TEA CO., INC., Home Office, BARRINGTON, ILLINOIS**

*"The Most Complete Coffee Service in America"*

14

# Part I: Dinnerware

Hall began producing decal pattern dinnerware in 1936. The four styles of dinnerware in this guide include:

**D-style**. This was the most commonly used shape of dinnerware. The plates are round and the cups and gravy boat have ear-shaped handles. The dinnerware consists of the following thirteen pieces:

| | |
|---|---|
| Bowl, 5¼″ | Plate, 6″ |
| Bowl, 6″ cereal | Plate, 8″ |
| Bowl, 8½″ flat soup | Plate, 9″ |
| Bowl, 9″ salad | Platter, 11¼″ oval |
| Bowl, 9″ round vegetable | Platter, 13¼″ oval |
| Cup | Saucer |
| Gravy boat | |

**C-style**. The C-style pieces are similar in shape to the D-style. However, all the C-style dinnerware is embossed with the "Radiance" design. The cup does not have an ear-shaped handle and there is no gravy boat.

**Ruffled D-style**. This is a modified D-style. The flat pieces and the bowls have a scallopped edge instead of just being plain round. Two additional size plates were included--a 10″ dinner and a 7¼″ salad plate.

**E-style**. The E-style dinnerware was designed by J. Palin Thorley and was produced during the forties and early fifties. Mount Vernon, Richmond, and Monticello, which were made for Sears, used this shape dinnerware. For a complete list of the pieces see the price listing in these patterns.

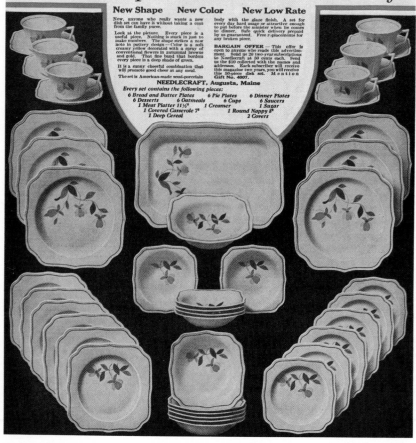

# Autumn Leaf

The Autumn Leaf pattern was introduced in 1933. Hall produced this pattern for the Jewel Tea Company of Chicago. Originally, the pattern was unnamed, but by 1942 it was called Autumn. In 1969, the name was officially changed to Autumn Leaf. Autumn Leaf was Hall's largest and longest running premium line.

Even though Autumn Leaf is widely collected and much has been written about the pattern, previously undiscovered pieces of Hall origin are still surfacing. Found recently were a pair of "Silhouette" style shakers and a morning tea set. Pieces like this were not production items and very few, if any, more will ever be found. They were either samples which were rejected, or were some decorator's private project.

Since Autumn Leaf was a premium line, new items were added yearly, and old ones were discontinued periodically. This gave customers incentive to buy products so they could obtain the premiums while they were still available. Items which were not popular as premiums were short-lived and are difficult for collectors to find today.

Although the Autumn Leaf decal was a Jewel Tea exclusive, non-Hall pieces may be found with this decal. Prior to 1933, the decal was used in a premium offer by Needlecraft magazine. This offer is shown in the photo to the left. The china is of unknown manufacture and the entire set could be obtained for twenty two-year subscriptions to the magazine at fifty cents each.

Other pieces with the Autumn Leaf decal include items made by Columbia, Crooksville, Harker, and Paden City. Some of these pieces may have been made before 1933, or they may have been samples which were submitted to Jewel Tea in an attempt to gain their business. It is easy to tell these pieces were not made by Hall. They are usually crazed and do not approach the Hall pieces in overall quality. They are of some interest to collectors as an oddity, but rarely sell for more than an equivalent Hall piece.

# Autumn Leaf Dinnerware

Autumn Leaf cream soups and St. Denis cups and saucers are not easily found in good condition. The 10″ dinner plate and the 6″ cereal bowls are eagerly sought after. The remainder of the pieces in this photograph are considered common by most collectors. As a result, many prudent shoppers demand perfect glaze and excellent gold on their dinnerware.

| | Item | Introduced | Discontinued | Price |
|---|---|---|---|---|
| Row 1: | Cup, ruffled-D | 1936 | 1976* | 4.50-5.00 |
| | Saucer, ruffled-D | 1936 | 1976* | 2.00-2.50 |
| | Cup, St. Denis | 1942 | 1976* | 10.00-12.00 |
| | Saucer, St. Denis | 1942 | 1976* | 4.00-5.00 |
| | Cream soup, ruffled-D | 1950 | 1976 | 14.00-16.00 |
| | Custard, "Radiance" | 1936 | 1976 | 3.00-4.00 |
| Row 2: | Bowl, salad | 1937 | 1976 | 10.00-12.00 |
| | Bowl, 8½″ flat soup | 1938 | 1976 | 8.00-12.00 |
| | Bowl, 6½″ cereal | 1938 | 1976 | 6.00-8.00 |
| | Bowl, 5½″ fruit | 1936 | 1976* | 3.00-4.00 |
| Row 3: | Plate, 10″ | 1938 | 1976* | 6.00-8.00 |
| | Plate, 9″ | 1936 | 1976 | 3.50-4.00 |
| | Plate, 8″ | 1938 | 1976 | 6.00-8.00 |
| Row 4: | Plate, 7¼″ | 1938 | 1976 | 4.00-5.00 |
| | Plate, 6″ | 1938 | 1976 | 2.00-2.50 |
| | Platter, 9″ oval | 1942 | 1976 | 10.00-12.00 |
| Row 5: | Platter, 11½″ oval | 1938 | 1976 | 11.00-12.00 |
| | Platter, 13½″ oval | 1938 | 1976 | 12.00-14.00 |

*Reissued later (1978)

# Autumn Leaf Dinnerware

The ruffled-D round vegetable bowl had a very short production of only two years. Therefore, it is not easily found. Although the divided oval vegetable bowl was listed in the catalogue for twenty years, it must not have been a good seller since it is very hard to find today. Even though the pie server shown is not a Hall item it is a desirable piece.

The "Rayed" sugar and creamer are not as easy to find as the newer ruffled-D sugar and creamer. Beware of buying sugar lids which have had the knobs glued back on. This seems to be a rather common problem with the sugar and condiment lids.

| Item | Introduced | Discontinued | Price |
|---|---|---|---|
| Row 1: Mug, Irish coffee | 1966 | 1976 | 40.00-45.00 |
| Mug, conic | 1966 | 1976 | 18.00-20.00 |
| Sugar and lid, "Rayed" | 1934 | 1940 | 10.00-12.00 |
| Creamer, "Rayed" | 1934 | 1940 | 5.00-6.00 |
| Row 2: Shaker, range, pr. | 1936 | 1976 | 12.00-14.00 |
| Drip jar | 1936 | 1976 | 9.00-11.00 |
| Sugar and lid, ruffled-D | 1940 | 1976 | 9.00-11.00 |
| Creamer, ruffled-D | 1940 | 1976 | 4.00-5.00 |
| Row 3: Bowl, covered oval, ruffled-D | 1940 | 1976 | 28.00-32.00 |
| Gravy boat, ruffled-D | 1940 | 1976 | 18.00-20.00 |
| Shaker, ruffled base, pr. | 1939 | 1976 | 8.00-10.00 |
| Row 4: Bowl, oval | 1939 | 1976* | 12.00-14.00 |
| Bowl, oval, divided | 1957 | 1976 | 40.00-45.00 |
| Row 5: Bowl, 9″ round | 1937 | 1939 | 35.00-40.00 |
| Cakeplate | 1937 | 1976 | 8.00-9.00 |
| Pie lifter | | | 40.00-45.00 |

*Reissued later (1978)

"Medallion" shape Autumn Leaf shakers.

20

SALT

PEPPER

# Autumn Leaf Kitchenware

The one-handle New England bean pot with the Autumn Leaf decal is unusual. The 2-pint diagonal-fluted french baker and the Fort Pitt individual baker are not easily found. The three-piece mixing bowl set was one of the longest running items in the Autumn Leaf line--originating in 1933 and continuing until the end.

| | Item | Introduced | Discontinued | Price |
|---|---|---|---|---|
| Row 1: | Bean pot, 1-handle 2¼ qt. | | | 175.00-200.00 |
| | Bean pot, 2-handle | 1960 | 1976 | 55.00-65.00 |
| Row 2: | Baker, french, 3 pt. | 1936 | 1976 | 9.00-11.00 |
| | Baker, french, 2 pt. | 1966 | 1976 | 20.00-22.00 |
| | Baker, french, 10 oz. | 1966 | 1976* | 5.00-6.00 |
| Row 3: | Casserole, round 2 qt. | 1935 | 1976 | 16.00-18.00 |
| | Pie plate | 1937 | 1976 | 16.00-18.00 |
| | Baker, Fort Pitt 12 oz. | 1966 | 1976 | 50.00-60.00 |
| Row 4: | Bowl, "Radiance" #5 | 1933 | 1976 | 12.00-14.00 |
| | Bowl, "Radiance" #4 | 1933 | 1976 | 10.00-12.00 |
| | Bowl, "Radiance" #3 | 1933 | 1976 | 9.00-10.00 |

*Reissued later (1978)

# Autumn Leaf Kitchenware

A big-eared cookie jar (sometimes referred to as a bean pot) was added to the Autumn leaf line in 1957. The shape was originally used in a line of Hall kitchenware designed by Eva Ziesel. The "Sundial" batter jug with the Autumn Leaf decal is very unusual and quite rare. Only a handful of these have been found. The "Rayed" cookie jar was only made for a short time and is not easily found. The stack set consists of one lid and three stacking units. Each set should have an 18 oz., 24 oz., and 34 oz. part.

The tidbit trays were made from regular ruffled-D style plates. However, in original Hall-produced tidbits, the backstamp is off-center and will not have a hole drilled through for the center handle.

| | Item | Introduced | Discontinued | Price |
|---|---|---|---|---|
| Row 1: | Cookie jar, Ziesel | 1957 | 1969 | 55.00-60.00 |
| | Cookie jar, "Rayed" | 1936 | 1939 | 60.00-70.00 |
| | Stack set | 1951 | 1976 | 42.00-47.00 |
| Row 2: | Ball jug #3 | 1938 | 1976 | 14.00-16.00 |
| | Batter jug, "Sundial" | | | 400.00-500.00 |
| | Jug, 2½ pt. "Rayed" | 1937 | 1976 | 10.00-12.00 |
| Row 3: | Tidbit, 3-tier | 1954 | 1969 | 35.00-40.00 |
| | Tidbit, 2-tier | 1954 | 1969 | 30.00-35.00 |

# Autumn Leaf Coffee Pots and Teapots

A nine cup, 9″ coffee pot was introduced in 1934. This pot utilized a metal dripper already in the Jewel line which did not have the leaf motif. In 1936, an 8 cup coffee maker with a plain straight-sided metal drip was added. The china lid to the coffee pot did not fit the metal drip. In 1937, a metal drip with a leaf motif was added to the original 8 cup base. This new dripper was designed to accept the china coffee pot lid. During the war years, a clear glass dripper was used to replace the metal drippers on the 8 cup "Rayed" coffee pots.

Since it was only in production for two years, the Newport teapot from the 1930's is not easily found. The old teapot has no gold around the tip of the spout, the decal is larger, and the hole in the lid is to the side of the knob. The later issue Newport (1978) has gold around the tip of the spout, has a smaller decal with a pink leaf, and the hole in the lid is in the front of the knob. The original Newport teapot was replaced by the longspout "Rayed" teapot in 1935.

| | Item | Introduced | Discontinued | Price |
|---|---|---|---|---|
| Row 1: | Coffee pot, "Rayed" 9 cup | 1934 | 1941 | 35.00-40.00 |
| | Coffee pot, "Rayed" 8 cup | 1936 | 1937 | 30.00-35.00 |
| | Coffee pot, "Rayed" 8 cup | 1937 | 1976 | 25.00-30.00 |
| Row 2: | Electric Percolator | 1957 | 1969 | 150.00-175.00 |
| | Drip coffee, all china | 1942 | 1945 | 135.00-140.00 |
| | Teapot, "Rayed" | 1935 | 1942 | 30.00-35.00 |
| Row 3: | Teapot, Newport, 30's | 1933 | 1935 | 70.00-75.00 |
| | Teapot, Newport, 70's | 1978 | 1978 | 60.00-65.00 |
| | Teapot, Aladdin | 1942 | 1976 | 30.00-32.00 |

# Autumn Leaf Butters, Clocks and Accessories

The Autumn Leaf electric clock features a works without numbers. These parts had "HALL" imprinted across the face and were manufactured by several different makers. Hall mounted these movements in a cut-out cakeplate blank. The clocks were battery powered and could be hung on the wall or set on a table. The second type of clock, without the glass face, was awarded as a prize to Jewel salesmen for achieving outstanding sales goals. This clock is not easily found.

Although the mustard and marmalade sets were only produced for one year, they are not as hard-to-find as such a short production run would indicate.

The design of the pound butter proved to be impractical and this item was discontinued after only one season. This butter and the round warmer were very hard-to-find until a quantity of each was uncovered in an old warehouse. Since then they have been available at what is probably an inflated price. This discovery is being slowly absorbed into collections and the prices will undoubtedly rise again when this temporary surplus is eventually absorbed. The round warmer was designed to be used with the round covered casserole and the oval warmer was used with the Aladdin teapot.

The one-quarter pound butter, introduced in 1961, replaced the one pound butter. The most common style butter has a scallopped knob. The other styles of ¼ pound butters are shown. They were never put into production and are seldom seen.

|  | Item | Introduced | Discontinued | Price |
|---|---|---|---|---|
| Row 1: | Butter, one pound | 1959 | 1960 | 115.00-125.00 |
|  | Butter, ¼ pound, wings |  |  | 300.00-350.00 |
|  | Butter, ¼ pound | 1961 | 1976 | 60.00-70.00 |
|  | Butter, straight knob (below) |  |  | 300.00-350.00 |
| Row 2: | Clock | 1956 | 1959 | 250.00-275.00 |
|  | Clock |  |  | 125.00-150.00 |
| Row 3: | Warmer, oval | 1955 | 1960 | 90.00-100.00 |
|  | Warmer, round | 1956 | 1960 | 75.00-85.00 |
|  | Marmalade, 3 pc. set | 1938 | 1939 | 42.00-47.00 |
|  | Mustard, 3 pc. set | 1938 | 1939 | 35.00-37.00 |
| Row 4: | Cakestand, metal base | 1958 | 1969 | 95.00-125.00 |
|  | Candy, metal base | 1958 | 1969 | 200.00-250.00 |
|  | Vase |  |  | 90.00-115.00 |

# Autumn Leaf Paper and Plastic Articles

The hotpad introduced in 1937 was cardboard with a tin back. Another hotpad, which was produced later and is hard-to-find, had a creamy wax-like coating and a red or green felt backing. The original shelf paper was 9¼″ wide and 9′ long. It had a design on the edge only. In 1956, shelf paper was again in the catalogue. This newer paper was 13″ wide and had an all-over pattern.

Plastic covers for bowls and small kitchen appliances were introduced in 1950. The bowl set consisted of eight pieces. There were seven assorted bowl covers and a draw-string plastic storage bag. Other plastic covers included a toaster cover, a standard-size mixer cover, and a Mary Dunbar mixer cover.

| Item | Introduced | Discontinued | Price |
|---|---|---|---|
| Coaster, 3¹/₈″ | | | 3.00-3.50 |
| Hotpad, 10¾″ oval | | | 8.00-9.50 |
| Hotpad, 7¼″ felt back | 1946 | | 11.00-12.00 |
| Mixer cover, standard | 1950 | 1961 | 20.00-25.00 |
| Mixer cover, Mary Dunbar | 1950 | 1961 | 20.00-25.00 |
| Plastic bowl covers, 8 pc. set | 1950 | 1961 | 80.00-85.00 |
| Playing cards, regular deck | 1943 | 1946 | 125.00-150.00 |
| Playing cards, Pinochle deck | 1943 | 1946 | 135.00-155.00 |
| Toaster cover | 1950 | 1961 | 20.00-25.00 |

Other plastic and paper accessories not pictured:

| | | | |
|---|---|---|---|
| Hotpad, 7¼″ tin back | 1937 | | 8.00-9.50 |
| Place mat, plastic | 1940 | | 18.00-20.00 |
| Shelf paper, pattern on edge | 1945 | | 10.00-12.00 sheet |
| Shelf paper, all-over pattern | 1956 | 1957 | 30.00-35.00 roll |

# Autumn Leaf Linen and Silverware

The muslin tablecloth and napkins introduced in 1937 were issued as a set. The Autumn motif ran just above a row of stripes along the edge. The pattern was repeated again in the center of the cloth.

The two sizes of tablecloth offered in 1950 were cotton with a plastic coating. The pattern had been changed to an all-over Autumn Leaf design.

In 1955, a cotton sailcloth tablecloth was introduced in two sizes. This tablecloth features a border design only. This consists of a gold stripe below the Autumn pattern.

Curt-towels could be used as both curtains and tea towels. They incorporated both the Autumn Leaf design and a clock motif.

The silverware offered in 1958 was a Jewel exclusive made by the International Silver Company. The sets were offered in a 24-piece service for six and a 50-piece service for eight. Serving pieces which included a gravy ladle, meat fork, berry spoon and a sugar shell were also available.

| Item | Introduced | Discontinued | Price |
|------|-----------|--------------|-------|
| Curt-towels, 4 pc set | 1957 | 1959 | 30.00-38.00 |
| Napkins, 16″ square | 1937 | 1942 | 35.00-40.00 |
| Silverware, silverplate | | | |
| 24 pc. set | 1958 | 1959 | 350.00-450.00 |
| Silverware, stainless | | | |
| 24 pc. set | 1960 | 1968 | 175.00-200.00 |
| Tablecloth, muslin | | | |
| 56x81 | 1937 | 1942 | 150.00-175.00 |
| Tablecloth, plastic | | | |
| 54x54 | 1950 | 1953 | 65.00-70.00 |
| Tablecloth, plastic | | | |
| 54x72 | 1950 | 1953 | 80.00-90.00 |
| Tablecloth, sailcloth | | | |
| 54x54 | 1955 | 1958 | 65.00-70.00 |
| Tablecloth, sailcloth | | | |
| 54x72 | 1955 | 1958 | 75.00-85.00 |
| Tea towel 16″x33″ | 1956 | 1957 | 20.00-25.00 |

# Autumn Leaf Tin Accessories

Many Hall China collectors seem to be quite content to live without any metal Autumn Leaf accessories. However, there is enough interest in these metal items to insure that all but the most worn will eventually find a home in someone's china cabinet. Be aware that the finish on these tin pieces practically vanishes at the sight of water. Another frequent cause of damage is caused by placing price stickers or tape over the finish. When the tag is removed the paint comes off also.

The thermos is found infrequently. Production was curtailed due to the restrictions imposed during WWII. The cleanser can and the sifter are two pieces which many collectors are still trying to find. The square canisters are a later issue than the round ones, but they don't seem to turn up as often. The plastic knobs on the square canisters tend to be easily damaged.

| | Item | Introduced | Discontinued | Price |
|---|---|---|---|---|
| Row 1: | Canister, 8¼″ sugar | 1959 | | 18.00-20.00 |
| | Canister, 8¼″ flour | 1959 | | 18.00-20.00 |
| | Canister 4″ tea | 1959 | | 15.00-18.00 |
| | Canister, 4″ coffee | 1959 | | 15.00-18.00 |
| | Cleanser can | | | 125.00-150.00 |
| Row 2: | Canister, round, tall | 1935 | 1942 | 22.00-25.00 |
| | Canister, round, med. | 1935 | 1942 | 16.00-18.00 |
| | Canister, round, small | 1935 | 1942 | 12.00-14.00 |
| | Sifter | | | 75.00-85.00 |
| Row 3: | Canister, round, tall (gold lid) | 1960 | 1962 | 14.00-16.00 |
| | Canister, round, short (gold lid) | 1960 | 1962 | 10.00-12.00 |
| | Thermos | 1941 | 1941 | 145.00-165.00 |

# Autumn Leaf Tin Accessories

Metal accessories were easily damaged through use and by washing. This damage drastically reduces the desirability and value of the piece. Many collectors will not consider buying even an unusual piece of tinware unless it is in an "almost mint" condition.

The early cakesafe has the pattern on the sides and the top of the lid; the later cakesafe only has the design on the side of the lid.

Use care when cleaning the glass trays. The paint under the glass is easily damaged by water. Even a small amount of wrinkling in the paint will reduce the value.

Quite a few of the bread boxes have been turning up in their original boxes. These are especially desirable since they usually have not been used and are in "like new" condition.

| Item | Introduced | Discontinued | Price |
|---|---|---|---|
| Row 1: Glass tray | 1975 | 1976 | 55.00-60.00 |
| Row 2: Coffee dispenser | 1941 | 1941 | 45.00-50.00 |
| Bread Box | 1937 | 1942 | 100.00-125.00 |
| Row 3: Cakesafe | 1935 | 1941 | 27.00-32.00 |
| Cakesafe | 1950 | 1953 | 15.00-17.00 |
| Metal accessories not pictured: | | | |
| Tray, 18¾" oval | 1934 | 1938 | 32.00-35.00 |
| Tray, rectangular, (red border) | | | 35.00-45.00 |
| Chair, kitchen | 1939 | 1942 | 450.00-500.00 |

# Recent Bakeware and Non-Hall Autumn Leaf

The photograph to the right shows a recent cookware and bakeware premium of the Jewel Company. Most people are not yet interested in collecting items which are this new. However these are probably pieces which will be sought after in the future.

The picture below shows the Autumn Leaf decal on a pottery which was not produced by Hall.

# Autumn Leaf Glass and Metal Accessories

With the exception of the tumblers, most of the items on this page are not very popular with Hall collectors. Most of these articles are later Jewel premiums and do not bear much resemblance to the Autumn Leaf design used on the Hall china.

The candlesticks in the third row were also used as the base for the footed cake plate and the footed candy. These are pictured on page 29.

The Glasbake articles in the last two rows are part of a short-lived 9-piece bakeware set introduced in 1961. The set consisted of a divided oval vegetable, two sizes of covered casseroles, and a four piece bowl set. These pieces were not popular and were dropped after one season.

| Item | Introduced | Discontinued | Price |
|---|---|---|---|
| Row 1: Tumbler, frosted, banded | | | 20.00-22.00 |
| Tumbler, 5½" frosted | 1940 | 1949 | 11.00-13.00 |
| Tumbler, 3¾" frosted | 1950 | 1953 | 18.00-20.00 |
| Tumbler, 16 oz. Brockway | 1975 | 1976 | 18.00-20.00 |
| Tumbler, 13 oz. Brockway | 1975 | 1976 | 14.00-16.00 |
| Tumbler, 9 oz. Brockway | 1975 | 1976 | 15.00-18.00 |
| Row 2: Tumbler, 15 oz. Libbey | 1960 | 1961 | 22.00-25.00 |
| Tumbler, 10 oz. Libbey | 1958 | 1961 | 20.00-22.00 |
| Tumbler, 10 oz. ftd. Libbey | 1960 | 1961 | 20.00-22.00 |
| Tumbler, 6½ oz. ftd. Libbey | 1960 | 1961 | 15.00-18.00 |
| Sauce dish, Douglas | 1961 | 1962 | 15.00-20.00 |
| Warmer base | 1961 | 1962 | 5.00-8.00 |
| Row 3: Percolator, Douglas | 1961 | 1962 | 25.00-30.00 |
| Canister, brown and gold | | | 5.00-8.00 |
| Canister, white plastic lid | | | 7.00-9.00 |
| Candlestick, pair | | | 25.00-30.00 |
| Row 4: Casserole, Glasbake | 1961 | 1962 | 9.00-11.00 |
| Divided bowl, Glasbake | 1961 | 1962 | 9.00-11.00 |
| Bowl set, 4 pc. Glasbake | 1961 | 1962 | 22.00-25.00 |
| Casserole bottom, Glasbake | 1961 | 1962 | 5.00-6.00 |
| Not pictured: Hurricane lamp, Douglas, pair | 1961 | 1962 | 25.00-30.00 |

# Blue Bouquet

Blue Bouquet was a premium line Hall produced for the Standard Coffee Company of New Orleans from the early fifties through the midsixties. Therefore this pattern is more abundant in the South. The dinnerware consists of the complete D-style. Many china accessory pieces and a few metal items have also been found.

Hard-to-find pieces include the pretzel jar, the New England bean pot #4, the electric percolator, the "Thick Rim" soup tureen, and the leftovers. The electric percolator has a specially designed heating element which fits between the coffee base and the dripper.

A few metal items including canisters and a coffee dispenser have surfaced.

| D-style Dinnerware | Price |
|---|---|
| Bowl, 5½″ fruit | 3.50-4.00 |
| Bowl, 6″ cereal | 4.50-5.50 |
| Bowl, 8½″ flat soup | 10.00-12.00 |
| Bowl, 9″ salad | 12.00-14.00 |
| Bowl, 9¼″ round vegetable | 20.00-22.00 |
| Cup | 4.00-5.50 |
| Gravy boat | 20.00-22.00 |
| Plate, 6″ | 2.00-2.50 |
| Plate, 8¼″ | 3.50-4.00 |
| Plate, 9″ | 4.50-5.00 |
| Platter, 11¼″ oval | 14.00-16.00 |
| Platter, 13¼″ oval | 16.00-18.00 |
| Saucer | 1.50-2.00 |

**Row 1:** Sugar and creamer, Boston; salad bowl, 9″; sugar and creamer, modern. **Row 2:** Drip jar, "Thick Rim"; salt and pepper, handled; cup and saucer. **Row 3:** Bowl, flat soup; bowl, 6″ cereal; bowl, 5³/₄″ fruit. **Row 4:** Plate, 9″ dinner; plate, 8¹/₄″; plate, 6″. **Row 5:** Platter, 13″ oval; bowl, 7³/₄″ flared; custard, "Thick Rim".

# Blue Bouquet

| China Accessory Items | Price |
|---|---|
| Ball jug #3 | 22.00-25.00 |
| Baker, french flute | 13.00-14.00 |
| Bean pot, New England #4 | 42.00-47.00 |
| Bowl, 7¾″ flared | 18.00-20.00 |
| Bowl 6″ "Thick Rim" | 8.00-10.00 |
| Bowl 7½″ "Thick Rim" | 14.00-16.00 |
| Bowl 8½″ "Thick Rim" | 15.00-17.00 |
| Bowl 6″ "Radiance" #3 | 7.00-9.00 |
| Bowl, 7½″ "Radiance" #4 | 11.00-12.00 |
| Bowl, 9″ "Radiance" #5 | 13.00-15.00 |
| Cakeplate | 11.00-12.00 |
| Casserole, "Thick Rim" | 25.00-30.00 |
| Casserole, "Radiance" | 27.00-30.00 |
| Coffee pot, "Five Band" | 45.00-47.00 |
| Coffee pot, "Terrace" | 42.00-45.00 |
| Creamer, Boston | 6.00-7.00 |
| Creamer, modern | 6.00-7.00 |
| Custard | 3.50-4.50 |
| Drip jar, "Thick Rim" | 16.00-18.00 |
| Electric percolator | 95.00-110.00 |
| Jug, "Medallion" #3 | 14.00-16.00 |
| Leftover, rectangular | 22.00-25.00 |
| Leftover, square | 32.00-35.00 |
| Pie Plate | 14.00-16.00 |
| Pretzel jar | 50.00-55.00 |
| Shakers, teardrop, pr. | 14.00-16.00 |
| Shakers, handled, pr. | 14.00-16.00 |
| Spoon | 32.00-35.00 |
| Soup tureen | 55.00-65.00 |
| Sugar and lid, Boston | 10.00-12.00 |
| Sugar and lid, modern | 10.00-12.00 |
| Teapot, Aladdin | 40.00-45.00 |

| Metal Accessories | Price |
|---|---|
| Canister | 10.00-12.00 |
| Coffee dispenser | 12.00-14.00 |

**Row 1:** Pretzel jar; bean pot, New England #4; coffee pot, "Terrace". **Row 2:** Ball jug #3; teapot with infusor, Aladdin; coffee pot, "Five Band". **Row 3:** Soup tureen; jug, "Medallion" #3; casserole, "Thick Rim". **Row 4:** Electric percolator; coffee dispenser; metal canisters.

# Crocus

Crocus was a Hall dinnerware line introduced in the mid-thirties. Hunting for the complete D-style dinnerware service as well as the multitude of china and metal accessory pieces provides collectors with a challenge.

Rare pieces include the "Zephyr" style one pound butter, the "Zephyr" style leftover, and "Zephyr" style water bottle. Hard-to-find pieces are the soup tureen with either the clover or plain style lid, the New England bean pot, the all-china Drip-O-lator, the "Simplicity" jug, the pretzel jar, and the "Radiance" stack set. The beverage mug and the #1188 open drip jar are still lacking from many collections also.

| D-style Dinnerware | Price |
| --- | --- |
| Bowl, 5½″ fruit | 2.50-3.00 |
| Bowl, 6″cereal | 5.00-6.00 |
| Bowl, 8½″ flat soup | 10.00-12.00 |
| Bowl, 9″ salad | 12.00-14.00 |
| Bowl, 9″ round vegetable | 14.00-16.00 |
| Bowl, oval | 12.00-14.00 |
| Cup | 5.00-6.00 |
| Gravy boat | 18.00-20.00 |
| Plate, 6″ | 2.00-2.50 |
| Plate, 8¼″ | 3.50-4.00 |
| Plate, 9″ | 4.00-5.50 |
| Platter, 11¼″ oval | 12.00-14.00 |
| Platter, 13¼″ oval | 14.00-15.00 |
| Saucer | 1.50-2.00 |

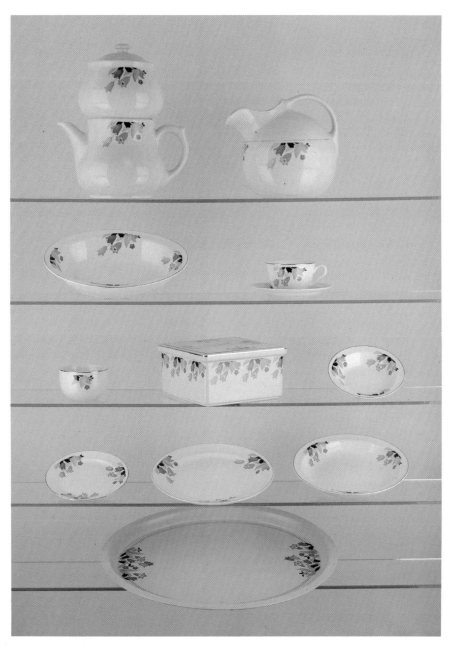

**Row 1:** All-china coffee pot, Drip-O-lator; ball jug #3. **Row 2:** Bowl, 9″ round; cup and saucer. **Row 3:** Custard, "Radiance"; leftover, square; bowl, 5½″ fruit. **Row 4:** Plate, 6″; plate, 9″; bowl, flat soup. **Row 5:** Tray, oval, metal.

# Crocus

| China Accessory Pieces | Price |
|---|---|
| Baker, french fluted | 16.00-18.00 |
| Ball jug #3 | 28.00-32.00 |
| Bean pot, New England #4 | 50.00-55.00 |
| Bowl, 6″ "Radiance" #3 | 8.00-10.00 |
| Bowl, 7½″ "Radiance" #4 | 10.00-12.00 |
| Bowl, 9″ "Radiance" #5 | 14.00-16.00 |
| Butter, one pound, "Zephyr"-style | 350.00-400.00 |
| Cakeplate | 13.00-14.00 |
| Casserole, "Radiance" | 22.00-25.00 |
| Coffee pot, "Medallion" | 35.00-40.00 |
| Coffee pot, crest, Drip-O-lator | 27.00-30.00 |
| Coffee pot, "Terrace" | 30.00-35.00 |
| Creamer, Art Deco | 6.50-7.50 |
| Creamer, "Medallion" | 6.50-7.50 |
| Creamer, modern | 6.50-7.50 |
| Custard | 3.50-4.00 |
| Dripolator, all-china | 95.00-110.00 |
| Drip jar, #1188 open | 22.00-25.00 |
| Drip jar, covered, "Radiance" | 16.00-18.00 |
| Jug, "Simplicity" | 75.00-85.00 |
| Leftover, "Zephyr"-style | 150.00-175.00 |
| Leftover, rectangular | 22.00-25.00 |
| Leftover, square | 28.00-30.00 |
| Mug, beverage | 25.00-27.00 |
| Pie plate | 12.00-14.00 |
| Pretzel jar | 50.00-55.00 |
| Shakers, handled, ea. | 7.00-8.00 |
| Soup tureen, plain or clover lid | 70.00-75.00 |
| Stack set, "Radiance" | 40.00-45.00 |
| Sugar and lid, Art Deco | 10.00-12.00 |
| Sugar and lid, "Medallion" | 10.00-12.00 |
| Sugar and lid, modern | 9.00-11.00 |
| Teapot, Boston | 25.00-30.00 |
| Teapot, "Medallion" | 22.00-25.00 |
| Teapot, New York | 25.00-27.00 |
| Tidbit tray, 3-tier | 32.00-35.00 |
| Water bottle, "Zephyr"-style | 95.00-110.00 |

| Metal Accessories | Price |
|---|---|
| Coffee dispenser | 10.00-12.00 |
| Tray, oval | 18.00-20.00 |

**Row 1:** Gravy boat; bean pot, New England #4; sugar, Art Deco style; creamer, Art Deco style. **Row 2:** Butter, "Zephyr"; leftover, "Zephyr"; leftover, rectangular. **Row 3:** Drip jar, "Radiance"; salt and pepper, handled; mug, beverage. **Row 4:** Teapot, New York; soup tureen; tidbit, 3-tier.

# Orange Poppy

Orange Poppy was introduced in 1933, and was produced through the fifties. The line was used as a premium for the Great American Tea Company and has numerous interesting pieces. Among the most difficult pieces to find are the spoon, the Melody teapot, the three-piece mustard set and the "Novelty" shakers. Metal pieces are also difficult to find in good condition. Items such as the bread box, soap dispenser, match box and the waste basket are seldom seen in any condition.

Orange Poppy dinnerware uses the C-style shape. All ten pieces are available in good supply, although the serving pieces are becoming more elusive.

| Orange Poppy Dinnerware | Price |
|---|---|
| Bowl, 5½" fruit | 3.50-4.00 |
| Bowl, 8½" flat soup | 10.00-12.00 |
| Bowl, 9" salad | 10.00-12.00 |
| Bowl, 9¼" round vegetable | 20.00-22.00 |
| Cup | 4.00-5.50 |
| Plate, 7" | 3.00-4.50 |
| Plate, 7¾" | 4.50-5.50 |
| Plate, 9" | 6.00-7.00 |
| Platter, 11¼" oval | 12.00-14.00 |
| Platter, 13¼" oval | 16.00-18.00 |
| Saucer | 1.50-2.00 |

**Row 1:** Sugar and creamer, "Great American"; mustard, 3 pc. set; custard. **Row 2:** Bowl, "Radiance" #5; bowl, 9″ round; bowl, 5¹/₂″ fruit. **Row 3:** Bowl, 9″ salad; cakeplate; plate, 9″ dinner. **Row 4:** Spoon; cup and saucer; salt and pepper, metal. **Row 5:** Canister set, 4 pc. metal.

# Orange Poppy

| Orange Poppy Accessory Pieces | Price |
|---|---|
| Baker, french flute | 11.00-13.00 |
| Ball jug #3 | 16.00-18.00 |
| Bean pot, New England #4 | 40.00-45.00 |
| Bowl, 6″ "Radiance" #3 | 7.00-9.00 |
| Bowl, 7½″ "Radiance" #4 | 9.00-11.00 |
| Bowl, 9″ "Radiance" #5 | 14.00-16.00 |
| Bowl, 10″ "Radiance" #6 | 20.00-22.00 |
| Cakeplate | 11.00-12.00 |
| Casserole, 8″ oval | 20.00-22.00 |
| Casserole, 11¼″ oval | 65.00-75.00 |
| Casserole, round | 20.00-22.00 |
| Coffee pot, "Great American" | 40.00-45.00 |
| Coffee pot, S-lid | 35.00-40.00 |
| Creamer, "Great American" | 8.00-9.00 |
| Custard | 3.50-4.50 |
| Drip jar, "Radiance" | 14.00-16.00 |
| Jug, "Radiance" #4 | 12.00-14.00 |
| Jug "Radiance" #5 | 16.00-18.00 |
| Leftover, loop handle | 28.00-30.00 |
| Pretzel jar | 50.00-55.00 |
| Shakers, teardrop, ea. | 6.00-8.00 |
| Shakers, handled, ea. | 8.00-9.00 |
| Shakers, "Novelty", ea. | 12.00-14.00 |
| Spoon | 35.00-40.00 |
| Sugar and lid, "Great American" | 12.00-14.00 |
| Teapot, Bellvue | 85.00-95.00 |
| Teapot, Boston | 32.00-37.00 |
| Teapot, Doughnut | 85.00-100.00 |
| Teapot, Melody | 85.00-95.00 |
| Teapot, Streamline | 45.00-50.00 |
| Teapot, Windshield | 65.00-75.00 |

| Metal Accessories | Price |
|---|---|
| Bread box | 45.00-50.00 |
| Canister set, 4 pc. | 35.00-40.00 |
| Coffee dispenser | 22.00-25.00 |
| Match box | 16.00-18.00 |
| Sifter | 18.00-20.00 |
| Soap dispenser | 30.00-35.00 |
| Waste basket | 20.00-25.00 |

**Row 1:** Coffee pot, S-lid; coffee pot, "Great American"; teapot, Bellvue. **Row 2:** Teapot, Melody; teapot, Doughnut; ball jug #3. **Row 3:** Pretzel jar; bean pot, New England #4; casserole, 8″ oval. **Row 4:** Salt, handled; drip jar, "Radiance"; pepper, handled; leftover, loop handle; canister, "Radiance".

# Pastel Morning Glory and Serenade

Very little information is available on Pastel Morning Glory. The pattern seems to have been of thirties origin and appears to have been most widely distributed in the upper Michigan and Wisconsin areas. The complete D-style dinnerware is available along with a moderate number of accessory pieces. The New England bean pot and the "Radiance" stack set appear to be more difficult to find, as is the dinnerware.

The Serenade pattern was distributed as a premium by the Chicago-based Eureka Tea Company. D-style dinnerware and a limited number of china accessory pieces are available. Of the known pieces, the pretzel jar is the hardest to find. Other items besides those listed should also exist.

The Art Deco sugar and the handled shakers in the bottom row of the photograph were also probably a premium item for Eureka. The pattern is not known, although it is similar to Eureka's Homewood pattern.

| D-style Dinnerware | Pastel Morning Glory | Serenade |
| --- | --- | --- |
| Bowl, 5½″ fruit | 4.50-5.50 | 3.00-3.50 |
| Bowl, 6″ cereal | 5.50-6.50 | 4.50-5.50 |
| Bowl, 8½″ flat soup | 10.00-12.00 | 9.00-11.00 |
| Bowl, 9″ salad | 12.00-14.00 | 9.00-11.00 |
| Bowl, 9″ round | 14.00-16.00 | 16.00-18.00 |
| Cup | 5.00-6.00 | 4.00-5.00 |
| Gravy boat | 20.00-22.00 | 18.00-20.00 |
| Plate, 6″ | 2.50-3.00 | 2.00-2.50 |
| Plate, 8¼″ | 3.50-4.50 | 3.00-4.00 |
| Plate, 9″ | 6.50-7.50 | 4.00-5.50 |
| Platter, 11¼″ | 14.00-16.00 | 12.00-14.00 |
| Platter, 13¼″ | 16.00-18.00 | 14.00-16.00 |
| Saucer | 1.50-2.00 | 1.50-2.00 |

| Pastel Morning Glory Accessory Pieces | Price | Serenade Accessory Pieces | Price |
| --- | --- | --- | --- |
| Ball jug #3 | 22.00-25.00 | Bowl, 6″ "Radiance" #3 | 6.00-8.00 |
| Bean pot, New Eng. #4 | 45.00-55.00 | Bowl, 7½″ "Rad- | |
| Bowl, oval | 14.00-16.00 | iance" #4 | 9.00-11.00 |
| Casserole, "Radiance" | 27.00-29.00 | Bowl, 9″ "Radiance" #5 | 12.00-14.00 |
| Creamer, modern | 7.00-9.00 | Casserole, "Radiance" | 22.00-25.00 |
| Drip, #1188 open | 15.00-18.00 | Coffee pot, | |
| Jug, "Radiance" #5 | 18.00-20.00 | "Terrace" | 16.00-18.00 |
| Shakers, handled, ea. | 9.00-11.00 | Pretzel jar | 45.00-50.00 |
| Stack set, "Radiance" | 30.00-35.00 | Shakers, handled, ea | 7.00-9.00 |
| Sugar & lid, modern | 12.00-14.00 | | |

Bean pot, New England #4; casserole lid, "Radiance"; salt and pepper, handled

**Row 1:** Jug, "Radiance" #5, Pastel Morning Glory; sugar and lid, modern, Pastel Morning Glory. **Row 2:** Bowl, 5¹/₂" fruit, Pastel Morning Glory; bowl, 8¹/₂" flat soup, Pastel Morning Glory; plate, 9" dinner, Pastel Morning Glory. **Row 3:** Bowl, "Radiance" #4, Serenade; salt and pepper, handled, Serenade. **Row 4:** Cup and saucer, Serenade; plate, 9" dinner, Serenade; platter, 11¹/₄", Serenade. **Row 5:** Sugar and lid, unknown; salt and pepper, handled, unknown.

# Red Poppy

Production of Red Poppy begain in the mid 1930's and continued for about twenty years. Red Poppy was a premium item for the Grand Union Tea Company and the popularity of this long-running line resulted in the addition of a variety of china and metal accessory pieces. The dinnerware shape was the D-style.

The Aladdin teapot and the fluted french baker with the Red Poppy decal were produced on a Hi-white body for some company other than Grand Union. The Red Poppy produced for Grand Union came on an ivory body.

The #1188 open drip is not often found. Other china pieces in this pattern seem to be readily available. Metal accessories with the Red Poppy decal were available in the 1940's through Montgomery Ward mail-order catalogues. These metal pieces did not hold up very well, and collectors are still turning down pieces that are less than perfect. Hard-to-find items include a dustpan, the soap dispenser, and the breadbox.

| Red Poppy Dinnerware | Price |
|---|---|
| Bowl, 5½" fruit | 3.50-4.50 |
| Bowl, 6" cereal | 4.00-6.00 |
| Bowl, 8½" flat soup | 10.00-12.00 |
| Bowl, 9" salad | 10.00-12.00 |
| Bowl, 9" round | 16.00-18.00 |
| Bowl, 10¼" oval | 16.00-18.00 |
| Cup | 5.00-6.00 |
| Gravy boat | 20.00-22.00 |
| Plate, 6" | 1.50-2.00 |
| Plate, 7" | 3.00-4.00 |
| Plate, 9¼" | 5.00-6.00 |
| Plate, 10¹/₈" | 7.00-8.00 |
| Platter, 11¼" oval | 13.00-15.00 |
| Platter, 13¼" oval | 16.00-18.00 |
| Saucer | 1.00-1.50 |

**Row 1:** Shakers, teardrop; creamer, modern; gravy boat; tumbler, 10 oz. frosted. **Row 2:** Cup and saucer (pattern outside); cup and saucer (pattern inside); bowl, 9″ salad; bowl, 9″ round. **Row 3:** Pie plate; cake plate; bowl, flat soup. **Row 4:** Plate, 6″; plate, 7″; plate, 9″. **Row 5:** Platter, 13¹/₄″; bowl, 6″ cereal; bowl, 5¹/₂″ fruit.

# Red Poppy

| China Accessory Pieces | Price |
|---|---|
| Baker, french, flute | 14.00-16.00 |
| Ball jug #3 | 25.00-27.00 |
| Bowl, 6″ "Radiance" #3 | 9.00-11.00 |
| Bowl, 7½″ "Radiance" #4 | 12.00-14.00 |
| Bowl, 9″ "Radiance" #5 | 15.00-18.00 |
| Cakeplate | 11.00-13.00 |
| Casserole, "Radiance" | 18.00-20.00 |
| Coffee pot, "Daniel" | 18.00-20.00 |
| Creamer, modern | 7.00-8.00 |
| Creamer, "Daniel" | 7.00-8.00 |
| Custard, "Radiance" | 3.00-4.00 |
| Drip, #1188 open | 28.00-30.00 |
| Drip, "Radiance" | 12.00-15.00 |
| Jug, "Radiance" #5 | 10.00-12.00 |
| Pie plate | 16.00-18.00 |
| Shaker, teardrop, ea. | 6.50-7.50 |
| Shaker, handled, ea. | 8.00-9.00 |
| Sugar and lid, modern | 10.00-12.00 |
| Sugar and lid, "Daniel" | 10.00-12.00 |
| Teapot, Aladdin | 35.00-40.00 |
| Teapot, New York | 35.00-40.00 |

**Row 1:** Coffee pot, "Daniel"; sugar and creamer, "Daniel"; jug, "Radiance" # 5. **Row 2:** Teapot, New York; teapot, Aladdin; salt, handled; drip jar, "Radiance"; pepper, handled. **Row 3:** Casserole, "Radiance"; baker, French; drip jar #1188 open; custard. **Row 4:** Bowl, "Radiance"#5; bowl, "Radiance" #4; bowl, "Radiance" #3.

# Red Poppy

A clear glass gallon jar with a screw lid and the Red Poppy design painted on in enamel is available. This jar has also been found with green enamel poppies. Two styles of frosted tumblers are seen. One style is slightly taller than the other, the flower is a little different and the bands around the top are different colors--one has red bands and the other black. The clear glass tumblers are seldom seen.

Plastic items include a clock and a bowl and mixer cover set.

| Glass Accessories | Price |
|---|---|
| Canister, gallon | 20.00-22.00 |
| Tumbler, clear | 16.00-18.00 |
| Tumbler, frosted, (2 styles) | 9.00-11.00 |

| Metal Accessories | Price |
|---|---|
| Bread box | 20.00-22.00 |
| Cake safe | 12.00-14.00 |
| Canister set, round 4 pc. | 20.00-25.00 |
| Canister set, square 4 pc. | 27.00-30.00 |
| Clock, metal, teapot shape | 40.00-45.00 |
| Coffee dispenser | 14.00-16.00 |
| Hot pad | 7.00-9.00 |
| Matchholder | 22.00-25.00 |
| Recipe box | 20.00-22.00 |
| Shaker, ea. | 4.00-5.00 |
| Sifter | 12.00-14.00 |
| Soap dispenser | 25.00-27.00 |
| Tray, rectangular | 16.00-18.00 |
| Tray, round | 10.00-12.00 |
| Waste can, round, cone shaped | 18.00-20.00 |
| Waste can, step-on | 25.00-27.00 |
| Wax paper dispenser | 30.00-32.00 |

| Plastic Accessories | Price |
|---|---|
| Bowl covers, 8 pc set | 35.00-40.00 |
| Clock, teapot shape | 45.00-50.00 |
| Mixer cover | 10.00-12.00 |
| Cutting board | 25.00-27.00 |
| Tablecloth, cotton | 60.00-65.00 |

**Row 1:** Cutting board; coffee dispenser; sifter. **Row 2:** Canister set, square; shaker, metal; hotpad. **Row 3:** Canister set, round; matchholder. **Row 4:** Waxed paper dispenser; tablecloth; recipe box. **Row 5:** Round tray; rectangular tray.

# Springtime, Wild Poppy, Mums, Floral Lattice, Black Beauty

Springtime is a colorful floral decal on a Hi-white body. Pieces of Springtime are not easily found, but the kitchenware is more abundant than the dinnerware.

The Wild Poppy decal is elusive. This decal dates to the thirties and was sold by Macy's, but was not an exclusive for them. No dinnerware is known, but numerous serving pieces and kitchen items exist. One of the more interesting finds has been the "Radiance" canister set and shakers. An interesting variation of this decal includes pieces with only poppies. A piece with this variation may be seen in the photograph. It is the "Radiance" custard in the middle of the third row.

Mums is probably a 1930's decal. Some pieces have been showing up, but the pattern seems to be hard to find except in the North Central states.

Very little Floral Lattice is available except for the "Five Band" syrup and the "Five Band" batter bowl.

The "Radiance" casserole on the right on the bottom shelf is "Stonewall". The "Medallion" juicer has also been found in this pattern.

**Row 1:** Ball jug #3, Springtime; teapot, French, Springime; cup and saucer, Springtime.
**Row 2:** Bowl, 5½″ fruit, Springtime; salt, handled, Springtime; drip jar, "Thick Rim", Springtime; pepper, handled, Springtime; dish, shirred egg, Black Beauty. **Row 3:** Baker, oval, "Wild Poppy"; jug, "Radiance" #4 "Wild Poppy"; custard, "Poppy" creamer (signed Alice Gallagher). **Row 4:** Casserole, "Medallion," "Mums"; teapot, "Rutherford," "Mums"; salt and pepper, handled, "Mums". **Row 5:** Batter bowl, "Five Band", "Floral Lattice"; syrup, "Five Band," "Floral Lattice"; casserole, "Radiance", "Stonewall".

# Springtime, Wild Poppy, Mums, Floral Lattice, Black Beauty

| D-style Dinneware | Springtime | Mums |
|---|---|---|
| Bowl, 5½″ fruit | 3.50-4.00 | 3.50-4.00 |
| Bowl, 6″ cereal | 5.00-6.00 | 5.00-6.00 |
| Bowl, 8½″ flat soup | 8.00-9.00 | 7.00-8.00 |
| Bowl, 9″ salad | 10.00-12.00 | 10.00-12.00 |
| Bowl, 9″ round | 14.00-16.00 | 16.00-18.00 |
| Cup | 4.00-5.00 | 4.00-5.00 |
| Gravy boat | 16.00-18.00 | |
| Plate, 6″ | 1.50-2.00 | 1.00-1.50 |
| Plate, 8¼″ | 3.50-4.00 | 3.00-3.50 |
| Plate, 9¼″ | 5.50-6.50 | 5.00-6.00 |
| Platter, 11¼″ oval | 12.00-14.00 | 12.00-14.00 |
| Platter, 13¼″ oval | 14.00-16.00 | 14.00-16.00 |
| Saucer | 1.00-1.50 | 1.00-1.50 |

| Kitchenware | Springtime | "Wild Poppy" | Mums |
|---|---|---|---|
| Ball jug #3 | 25.00-27.00 | | |
| Baker, oval | | 14.00-16.00 | |
| Bowl, "Radiance" #3,4,5;set | | 25.00-30.00 | |
| Bean pot, New England #3 | | 55.00-60.00 | |
| Cake plate | 10.00-12.00 | | |
| Canister, "Radiance" | | 60.00-70.00 | |
| Casserole, #101 oval | | 25.00-27.00 | |
| Casserole, "Thick Rim" | 22.00-25.00 | 25.00-27.00 | |
| Casserole, "Medallion" | | | 30.00-35.00 |
| Casserole, "Radiance" | | 28.00-30.00 | 30.00-32.00 |

| Kitchenware | Springtime | "Wild Poppy" | Mums |
|---|---|---|---|
| Creamer, "Medallion" | | | 6.00-7.00 |
| Creamer, Hollywood | | 7.00-9.00 | |
| Creamer, modern | 5.00-7.00 | | |
| Creamer, New York | | 5.00-7.00 | |
| Custard | 4.00-5.00 | | |
| Custard, "Radiance" #1 | | 4.00-5.00 | 3.00-4.00 |
| Drip coffee, all-china | 75.00-85.00 | | |
| Drip jar, "Thick Rim" | 12.00-14.00 | | |
| Jug, "Radiance" #2 | | 35.00-37.00 | |
| Jug, "Radiance" #6 | 20.00-25.00 | | |
| Onion soup, individual | | 14.00-16.00 | |
| Pie plate | 12.00-14.00 | | |
| Shakers, handled, ea. | 9.00-11.00 | | 11.00-13.00 |
| Shakers, "Radiance" | | 25.00-30.00 | |
| Stack set, "Radiance" | | | 45.00-47.00 |
| Sugar and lid, "Medallion" | | | 10.00-12.00 |
| Sugar and lid, modern | 10.00-12.00 | | |
| Sugar and lid, New York | | 9.00-11.00 | |
| Teapot, french | 42.00-47.00 | | |
| Teapot, New York, 4 cup | | 45.00-50.00 | |
| Teapot, New York, 6 cup | | 45.00-50.00 | |
| Teapot | | | 55.00-60.00 |
| Teapot, "Radiance" | | 80.00-85.00 | |
| Tea tile, 6" | | 30.00-32.00 | |

Black Beauty casserole, 32.00-37.00; shirred egg dish, 18.00-22.00

"Stonewall" "Radiance" casserole, 28.00-30.00; "Medallion" juicer, 350.00-400.00; "Radiance" #2 jug and lid, 45.00-50.00.
"Floral Lattice" Ball jug #3, 14.00-16.00; "Five Band" batter bowl, 28.00-30.00; "Five Band" syrup, 20.00-22.00.

# Silhouette

The "Silhouette" pattern was introduced in the 1930's. Both Hall and Taylor, Smith, and Taylor used this same decal on pieces which were sold to Cook Coffee and Standard Coffee to be used as premiums. Today the laurel style dinnerware of Taylor, Smith, and Taylor is found more easily than the Hall dinnerware. However, some of the lack of availability of the Hall dinnerware may be the result of more avid collecting of the Hall pieces, resulting in the Hall items being removed from the dealers tables quicker. The TS&T pieces remain behind, thus appearing to be more plentiful.

Hard-to-find items include the pretzel jar, the Twin-Tee set, the "Simplicity" jug, the all-china drip, and the tea tiles.

Metal accessories include a 17½" oval platter, coasters, a wall-hanging match safe, and a wooden handled whisk. Crystal 10 ounce tumblers and a glass gallon-size canister with the "Silhouette" decal exists. A rolling pin made by Harker China Company also matches this pattern.

Collectors should also be aware of a similar decal on pieces produced by the Crooksville China Company. On these pieces there is a dog sitting at the foot of the table. Hall pieces do not have the dog.

| D-style Dinnerware | Price |
|---|---|
| Bowl, 5½" fruit | 3.50-4.50 |
| Bowl, 6" cereal | 6.00-7.00 |
| Bowl, 8½" flat soup | 10.00-12.00 |
| Bowl, 9" salad | 9.00-11.00 |
| Bowl, 9" round | 14.00-16.00 |
| Cup | 6.00-7.00 |
| Plate, 6" | 2.00-3.00 |
| Plate, 8¼" | 4.00-5.00 |
| Plate, 9¼" | 6.00-7.5.0 |
| Platter, 11¼" oval | 12.00-14.00 |
| Platter, 13¼" oval | 18.00-20.00 |
| Saucer | 1.50-2.00 |

**Row 1:** Teapot, New York; coffee pot, "Five Band"; teapot, "Medallion". **Row 2:** Pretzel ar; sugar and creamer, "Medallion"; jug, "Medallion" #3. **Row 3:** Leftover, square; lef- over, rectangular; tea tile; bowl, 9″ salad. **Row 4:** Bowl, "Medallion" #5; bowl, "Medallion" 4; bowl, "Medallion" #3; custard.

| China Accessories | Price |
|---|---|
| Baker, french | 12.00-14.00 |
| Ball jug #3 | 30.00-35.00 |
| Bowl, 3⅝″ | 5.00-7.00 |
| Bowl, 7¾″ | 20.00-22.00 |
| Bowl, 9″ salad | 10.00-12.00 |
| Bowl, 6″ "Medallion" #3 | 10.00-12.00 |
| Bowl, 7¼″ "Medallion" #4 | 15.00-18.00 |
| Bowl, 8½″ "Medallion" #5 | 20.00-22.00 |
| Bowl, 6″ "Radiance" #3 | 8.00-10.00 |
| Bowl, 7½″ "Radiance" #4 | 12.00-14.00 |
| Bowl, 9″ "Radiance" #5 | 18.00-20.00 |
| Casserole, "Medallion" | 25.00-27.00 |
| Coffee pot, "Five Band" | 25.00-27.00 |
| Coffee pot, "Five Band" (clear dripper) | 65.00-75.00 |
| Coffee pot, "Medallion" | 25.00-30.00 |
| Coffee pot, all-china drip | 110.00-125.00 |
| Creamer, "Medallion" | 7.50-9.00 |
| Creamer, modern | 7.50-9.00 |
| Drip jar, "Medallion" | 14.00-16.00 |
| Jug, "Simplicity" | 55.00-60.00 |
| Jug, "Medallion" #3 | 18.00-20.00 |
| Jug, "Medallion" #4 | 22.00-25.00 |
| Leftover, rectangular | 18.00-20.00 |
| Leftover, square | 25.00-30.00 |
| Mug, beverage | 28.00-32.00 |
| Pretzel jar | 45.00-55.00 |
| Shakers, "Five Band", ea. | 7.00-8.00 |
| Shakers, "Medallion", ea. | 13.00-15.00 |
| Shakers, handled, ea. | 8.00-10.00 |
| Sugar and lid, "Medallion" | 12.00-14.00 |
| Sugar and lid, modern | 12.00-14.00 |
| Teapot, "Five Band" | 35.00-40.00 |
| Teapot, "Medallion" | 35.00-40.00 |
| Teapot, New York | 50.00-60.00 |
| Teapot Streamline | 50.00-55.00 |
| Tea tile | 80.00-90.00 |

Row 1: All-china drip; "Simplicity" jug. Row 2: Beverage mug; shakers, "Five Band"; salt, "Medallion"; drip jar, "Medallion"; pepper, "Medallion".

| Other Accessories | Price |
|---|---|
| Bread box | 65.00-75.00 |
| Coaster | 3.00-4.00 |
| Canister set, 4 pc. | 35.00-40.00 |
| Cake set | 27.00-30.00 |
| Match safe | 20.00-25.00 |
| Metal tray, oval | 25.00-28.00 |
| Metal tray, rectangular | 20.00-22.00 |
| Mirror | 65.00-75.00 |
| Pitcher, crystal, Federal | 90.00-100.00 |
| Pitcher, crystal, Macbeth-Evans shape | 95.00-110.00 |
| Rolling pin (not Hall) | 85.00-95.00 |
| Shakers, lg. metal | 20.00-25.00 |
| Shelf paper (30 ft. pack) | 40.00-50.00 |
| Tumber, 10 oz. crystal | 15.00-18.00 |
| Whisk, wooden handle | 45.00-55.00 |

# Tulip

The tulip pattern was used as a premium by the Cook Coffee Company. The dinnerware shape was D-style with a 10″ dinner plate and no 8¼″ plate. A flat cake plate and a rolling pin with this decal are often found. These items were made by Harker China Company. Other pieces with this decal which were made by Harker and are not often seen include a pie lifter and a spoon. Hall pieces which are unusual include the "Thick Rim" casserole, the St. Denis cup and saucer, and the "Radiance" stack set.

| D-style Dinnerware | Price |
|---|---|
| Bowl, 5½″ fruit | 3.00-3.50 |
| Bowl, 6″ cereal | 4.40-5.50 |
| Bowl, 8½″ flat soup | 9.00-11.00 |
| Bowl, 9″ salad | 9.00-11.00 |
| Bowl, 9″ round | 15.00-17.00 |
| Bowl, oval | 12.00-14.00 |
| Cup | 4.00-5.00 |
| Gravy boat | 16.00-18.00 |
| Plate, 6″ | 2.00-2.50 |
| Plate, 7″ | 3.00-4.00 |
| Plate, 9″ | 4.00-4.50 |
| Plate, 10″ | 6.00-8.00 |
| Platter, 11¼″ oval | 13.00-15.00 |
| Platter, 13¼″ oval | 16.00-18.00 |
| Saucer | 1.00-1.50 |

| China Accessories | Price |
|---|---|
| Baker, french | 14.00-16.00 |
| Bowl, 6″ "Thick Rim" | 8.00-10.00 |
| Bowl, 7½″ "Thick Rim" | 10.00-12.00 |
| Bowl, 8½″ "Thick Rim" | 12.00-14.00 |
| Bowl, 6″ "Radiance" #3 | 7.00-9.00 |
| Bowl, 7½″ "Radiance" #4 | 9.00-11.00 |
| Bowl, 9″ "Radiance" #5 | 12.00-14.00 |
| Casserole, "Thick Rim" | 25.00-27.00 |
| Casserole, "Radiance" | 27.00-32.00 |
| Coffee pot, "Perk" | 20.00-25.00 |
| Cup, St Denis | 14.00-16.00 |
| Creamer, modern | 6.00-8.00 |
| Custard | 4.00-5.00 |
| Drip jar, "Thick Rim" | 14.00-16.00 |
| Drip coffee, all-china | 75.00-80.00 |
| Saucer, St. Denis | 3.00-4.00 |
| Shakers, handled, ea. | 10.00-11.00 |
| Stack set, "Radiance" | 45.00-50.00 |
| Sugar and lid, modern | 12.00-14.00 |

**Row 1:** Drip coffee, all-china; coffee pot, "Perk". **Row 2:** Bowl, oval; sugar and lid, modern. **Row 3:** Cup and saucer; bowl, $5/_2''$ fruit; gravy boat. **Row 4:** Plate $6^1/_4''$; bowl, $8^1/_2''$ flat soup. **Row 5:** Plate, 10''; plate, 9''

# Wildfire

Wildfire was used as a premium by the Great American Tea Company in the 1950's. A modified D-style was used for the dinnerware. A 10" dinner plate, a 7¼" plate, and an oval vegetable bowl were added and the 8¼" plate was not produced. Unusual pieces include an egg cup and the "Pert" shakers and jug.

| D-style Dinnerware | Price |
|---|---|
| Bowl, 5½" fruit | 3.00-3.50 |
| Bowl, 6" cereal | 5.50-6.00 |
| Bowl, 8½" flat soup | 9.00-10.00 |
| Bowl, 9" salad | 9.00-10.00 |
| Bowl, 9" round | 14.00-16.00 |
| Bowl, oval | 12.00-14.00 |
| Cup | 4.00-5.00 |
| Gravy boat | 14.00-16.00 |
| Plate, 6" | 2.00-2.50 |
| Plate, 7" | 3.50-4.00 |
| Plate, 10" | 5.00-6.00 |
| Platter, 11¼" | 10.00-12.00 |
| Platter, 13¼" | 12.00-14.00 |
| Saucer | 2.00-2.50 |

| China Accessories | Price |
|---|---|
| Baker, French | 10.00-12.00 |
| Bowl, 6" "Thick Rim" | 8.00-10.00 |
| Bowl, 7½" "Thick Rim" | 10.00-12.00 |
| Bowl, 8½" "Thick Rim" | 12.00-14.00 |
| Bowl, straight-sided#3 | 7.00-9.00 |
| Bowl, straight-sided #4 | 9.00-12.00 |
| Bowl, straight-sided#5 | 12.00-14.00 |
| Casserole, "Thick Rim" | 22.00-25.00 |
| Casserole, tab-handled | 25.00-27.00 |
| Coffee pot, S-Lid | 27.00-30.00 |
| Creamer | 6.00-8.00 |
| Custard, straight-sided | 4.00-4.50 |
| Drip jar, "Thick Rim" | 14.00-16.00 |
| Egg cup | 27.00-30.00 |
| Jug, "Pert", 5" | 22.00-25.00 |
| Jug, "Radiance" #5 | 20.00-22.00 |
| Pie plate | 10.00-12.00 |
| Shakers, teardrop, ea. | 5.00-6.00 |
| Shakers, handled, ea. | 7.00-8.00 |
| Shakers, "Pert", ea. | 8.00-9.00 |

| | |
|---|---|
| Sugar and lid | 10.00-12.00 |
| Teapot, Aladdin | 32.00-37.00 |
| Tidbit 3-tier | 28.00-30.00 |

| **Metal Accessories** | **Price** |
|---|---|
| Coffee dispenser | 10.00-12.00 |

**Row 1:** Coffee pot, S-lid; teapot, Aladdin. **Row 2:** Casserole, tab-handled; shaker, "Pert"; drip jar, tab-handled; salt, handled. **Row 3:** Casserole, "Thick Rim"; tidbit, 3-tier; cup. **Row 4:** Bowl, $5^1/_2''$ fruit; gravy boat; bowl, $8^1/_2''$ flat soup.

# Yellow Rose

Yellow Rose was produced for the Eureka Tea Company of Chicago. Distribution of this pattern seems to be very regional, with most of the pieces being uncovered in the northern midwest area. The complete D-style should be available, although we have not yet seen every piece.

This decal is found on several shapes which are not common in other popular patterns. The "Norse" coffee pot (on the top shelf, left), the individual onion soup (between the handled shakers), and the "Dome" Drip-O-lator (not pictured) may have been designed exclusively for Eureka.

Hard-to-find items include the "Norse" coffee pot, the "Radiance" stack set, and the all-china drip coffee.

| D-style Dinnerware | Price |
|---|---|
| Bowl, 5½" fruit | 3.00-3.50 |
| Bowl, 6" cereal | 4.00-5.00 |
| Bowl, 8½" flat soup | 8.00-9.00 |
| Bowl, 9" salad | 10.00-12.00 |
| Cup | 4.00-5.00 |
| Gravy boat | 18.00-20.00 |
| Plate, 6" | 1.50-2.00 |
| Plate, 8¼" | 3.50-4.00 |
| Plate, 9" | 4.00-5.00 |
| Platter, 11¼" oval | 10.00-12.00 |
| Platter, 13¼" oval | 12.00-14.00 |
| Saucer | 1.50-2.00 |

| China Accessories | Price |
|---|---|
| Baker, french | 12.00-14.00 |
| Casserole, "Radiance" | 18.00-20.00 |
| Coffee pot, "Waverly" | 25.00-27.00 |
| Coffee pot, "Norse" | 40.00-45.00 |
| Coffee pot, "Dome" | 22.00-25.00 |
| Creamer, "Norse" | 6.00-8.00 |
| Custard, "Radiance" | 3.00-4.00 |
| Drip coffee, all-china | 75.00-85.00 |
| Onion soup | 20.00-22.00 |
| Shakers, handled, ea. | 9.00-11.00 |
| Stack set, "Radiance" | 45.00-50.00 |
| Sugar and lid, "Norse" | 10.00-12.00 |
| Teapot, New York | 32.00-35.00 |

**Row 1:** Drip coffee, "Norse"; teapot, New York; creamer and sugar, "Norse". **Row 2:** Salt, handled; drip jar; pepper, handled; platter, 11¹/₄″ oval. **Row 3:** Bowl, 6″ cereal; bowl, 5¹/₂″ fruit; bowl, 8¹/₂″ flat soup. **Row 4:** Plate, 9″ dinner; plate, 8¹/₄″; cup.

# Cameo Rose

Cameo Rose was a pattern Hall made exclusively for the Jewel Tea Company. It was first offered in the fifties and remained available until the early seventies. The pattern contains a rose bud in the center of the piece. This is accented by a leaf border and gold trim. The dinnerware shape is E-style.

| Cameo Rose | Price |
|---|---|
| Bowl, 5¼″ fruit | 2.00-2.50 |
| Bowl, 6¼″ cereal | 3.00-3.50 |
| Bowl, cream soup | 7.00-8.00 |
| Bowl, 8″ flat soup | 7.00-8.00 |
| Bowl, 9″ round vegetable | 10.00-12.00 |
| Bowl, 10½″ oval vegetable | 10.00-12.00 |
| Butter, ¼# | 30.00-32.00 |
| Casserole | 27.00-32.00 |
| Creamer | 6.00-7.00 |
| Cup | 4.50-5.00 |
| Gravy boat | 14.00-16.00 |
| Pickle dish, 9″ | 8.00-10.00 |
| Plate, 6½″ | 2.00-2.50 |
| Plate, 8″ | 2.50-3.00 |
| Plate, 9¼″ | 3.00-4.00 |
| Plate, 10″ | 4.00-6.00 |
| Platter, 11¼″ | 10.00-12.00 |
| Platter, 13¼″ | 12.00-14.00 |
| Saucer | 1.00-1.50 |
| Shakers, pr. | 14.00-16.00 |
| Sugar and lid | 12.00-14.00 |
| Teapot, 6 cup | 37.00-40.00 |
| Tidbit tray | 27.00-32.00 |

**Row 1:** Sugar; creamer; ¹/₄# butter; shakers. **Row 2:** Teapot; casserole. **Row 3:** Cup and saucer; bowl, 5¹/₄″ fruit; plate, 6¹/₂″. **Row 4:** Plate, 7³/₄″; plate, 10″.

# Mount Vernon

Mount Vernon was a decorated line utilizing the E-style dinnerware. This pattern was sold by Sears in the 1940's under the name "Granitone."

A standard 32-piece service for six sold for $6.79 and was the most expensive of the three Hall patterns carried in the Sears' catalogue. The designer of Mt. Vernon was J. Palin Thorley who also designed some of Hall's teapots.

White Granitone candlesticks--without decoration--were offered with the dinnerware. A pair cost $1.69. Individual pieces of the china could also be obtained as open stock items.

| Mount Vernon | Price |
|---|---|
| Bowl, 5¼" sauce | 2.50-3.00 |
| Bowl, 6" cereal | 3.00-4.00 |
| Bowl, flat soup | 4.00-6.00 |
| Bowl, oval | 6.00-8.00 |
| Bowl, covered vegetable | 10.00-12.00 |
| Creamer | 4.00-5.00 |
| Cup | 3.50-4.00 |
| Drip coffee, all-china | 35.00-40.00 |
| Gravy boat | 10.00-12.00 |
| Plate, 6" | 1.50-2.00 |
| Plate, 7¼" | 2.00-2.50 |
| Plate, 9¼" | 3.00-3.50 |
| Plate, 10" | 4.00-5.00 |
| Platter, 13" | 9.00-10.00 |
| Platter, 15½" | 10.00-12.00 |
| Saucer | 1.00-1.50 |
| Sugar and lid | 8.00-9.00 |
| Tureen, covered | 16.00-18.00 |

**Row 1:** Sugar and lid, Mt. Vernon; drip coffee, Mt. Vernon; creamer, Mt. Vernon. **Row 2:** Cup and saucer, Mt. Vernon; bowl, 8¹/₂″flat soup, Mt. Vernon; bowl, cereal, Mt. Vernon. **Row 3:** Platter, 15¹/₂″ Mt. Vernon; plate, 10″ dinner, Mt. Vernon. **Row 4:** Sugar and creamer, Heather Rose; bowl, oval, Heather Rose; gravy boat, Heather Rose.

# Richmond and Heather Rose

Richmond and Heather Rose were both E-style dinnerware patterns sold during the forties. Richmond was sold by Sears as were Mount Vernon and another E-style pattern--Monticello. A limited number of kitchenware accessory pieces will be found in both these patterns. The Washington style teapot is not very old. Additional Heather Rose items are shown on page 79.

| Item | Richmond | Heather Rose |
|------|----------|--------------|
| Bowl, 5¼″ sauce | 2.00-2.50 | 2.50-3.00 |
| Bowl, 6″ cereal | 3.00-3.50 | 3.50-4.00 |
| Bowl, flat soup | 4.00-6.00 | 5.00-7.00 |
| Bowl, 9″ salad | 8.00-10.00 | 9.00-11.00 |
| Bowl, oval | 6.00-8.00 | 7.00-9.00 |
| Bowl, covered vegetable | 10.00-12.00 | 12.00-14.00 |
| Coffee pot, "Terrace" | | 28.00-30.00 |
| Creamer | 4.00-4.50 | 4.00-5.00 |
| Cup | 3.50-4.00 | 3.50-4.50 |
| Gravy boat | 9.00-10.00 | 10.00-12.00 |
| Jug, "Radiance" | 10.00-12.00 | 10.00-12.00 |
| Pie plate | | 12.00-14.00 |
| Plate, 6″ | 1.00-1.50 | 1.00-1.50 |
| Plate, 7¼″ | 2.00-2.50 | 2.00-2.50 |
| Plate, 9¼″ | 3.00-3.50 | 3.00-4.00 |
| Plate, 10″ | 4.00-5.00 | 4.00-5.00 |
| Platter, 13″ | 9.00-10.00 | 10.00-11.00 |
| Platter, 15½″ | 10.00-12.00 | 12.00-14.00 |
| Saucer | 1.00-1.50 | 1.00-1.50 |
| Sugar and lid | 7.00-9.00 | 8.00-10.00 |
| Teapot, Washington | | 14.00-16.00 |
| Tureen, covered | 14.00-16.00 | 17.00-20.00 |

**Row 1:** Jug, "Radiance", Richmond; bowl, 9″ salad, Richmond. **Row 2:** Cup and saucer, Richmond; plate, 9$^1/_4$″, Richmond; bowl, 5$^1/_4$″ sauce, Richmond. **Row 3:** Cup and saucer, Heather Rose; plate, 7$^1/_4$″ Heather Rose; plate 10″, Heather Rose; bowl, 5$^1/_4$″ sauce, Heather Rose. **Row 4:** Pie plate, Heather Rose; jug, "Radiance", Heather Rose; bowl, 9″ salad, Heather Rose.

# Part II: Kitchenware

Hall introduced its first kitchenware line--"Medallion"--in 1932. The first colors were ivory and lettuce. The success of this line led to a more ambitious kitchenware marketing program. New lines and additional colors were introduced. Decals were also applied to both ivory and cobalt bodies and more new patterns of kitchenware were formed. Among the most popular of these decal lines were #488 and Blue Blossom. There are a large number of different pieces in both these patterns. However, most of the pieces are not readily found. This provides interesting and challenging collecting.

Also, many of the kitchenware shapes were later used to provide accessory pieces in the decal dinnerware lines. Since they are more plentiful in this form, these decal kitchenware items that match the dinnerware patterns are probably more familiar to us than their plain counterparts.

Generally, solid color kitchenware has not been as collectible or as expensive as the decal kitchenware. However, lately, there has been more interest and the price of the harder-to-find plain items has been increasing.

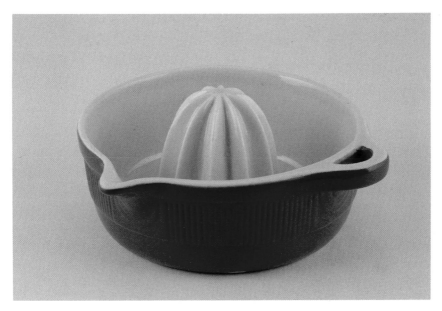

Chinese Red "Medallion" Juicer

# "Five Band" and "Sundial"

The "Five Band" kitchenware line was introduced in 1937. Chinese red was the most popular color then and is the most collectible color today. Other colors may be found including cobalt, Indian red, marine, cadet, ivory, and canary. The "Five Band" body was also used for a variety of decal lines. The hard-to-find Flamingo decal has been found on the batter bowl and the cookie jar. The casserole has two types of lids--knob handle and loop handle. The syrup has a lid and the teapot and coffee pot are the same shape. However, the coffee pot holds 9 cups and the teapot only holds 6 cups.

The success of the "Five Band" line brought about the introduction of the "Sundial" line in 1938. The casseroles, sugars and creamers, individual teapots, and individual coffee pots came in a number of sizes, some of which were made until recently. The most commonly found color is Chinese red. The hardest pieces to find include the cookie jar, coffee server, and the six cup teapot.

| Item | Red/Cobalt "Five Band" | Other Colors "Five Band" | Red/Cobalt "Sundial" | Other Colors "Sundial" |
|---|---|---|---|---|
| Batter jug | | | 60.00-65.00 | 40.00-45.00 |
| Batter bowl | 35.00-40.00 | 15.00-18.00 | | |
| Bowl, 6″ | 6.00-8.00 | 4.00-4.50 | | |
| Bowl, 7¼″ | 8.00-10.00 | 4.00-5.00 | | |
| Bowl, 8¾″ | 10.00-12.00 | 8.00-10.00 | | |
| Carafe | 55.00-60.00 | 40.00-45.00 | | |
| Casserole, #1, 4¾″ | | | 9.00-11.00 | 7.00-9.00 |
| Casserole, #2, 5¼″ | | | 10.00-12.00 | 8.00-10.00 |
| Casserole, #3, 6½″ | | | 10.00-12.00 | 8.00-10.00 |
| Casserole, #4, 8″ | 32.00-35.00 | *18.00-20.00 | 25.00-27.00 | 14.00-16.00 |
| Creamer | | | 6.00-7.00 | 4.00-5.00 |
| Coffee pot | 35.00-40.00 | 16.00-18.00 | | |
| Coffee pot, individual | | | 27.00-30.00 | 14.00-16.00 |
| Coffee server | | | 110.00-120.00 | |
| Cookie jar | 27.00-32.00 | **16.00-20.00 | 95.00-110.00 | |
| Shakers, ea. | 3.00-4.00 | 2.50-3.00 | | |
| Sugar | | | 6.00-7.00 | 3.50-4.00 |
| Syrup | 40.00-45.00 | 18.00-20.00 | 35.00-40.00 | 20.00-25.00 |
| Teapot, individual | | | 30.00-32.00 | 13.00-14.00 |
| Teapot, 6 cup | | | 55.00-60.00 | 40.00-45.00 |

*With Flamingo decal 25.00-27.00
**With Flamingo decal 45.00-50.00

**Row 1:** Cookie jar, "Five Band"; batter bowl, "Five Band"; shakers, "Five Band"; carafe, "Five Band". **Row 2:** Jug, 2 qt. "Five Band"; syrup, "Five Band"; bowl, 8³/₄″, "Five Band"; bowl, 6″, "Five Band". **Row 3:** Batter jug, "Sundial"; cookie jar, "Sundial"; creamer, individual, "Sundial"; sugar, individual, "Sundial"; creamer, individual, "Sundial". **Row 4:** Coffee server, "Sundial"; teapot, 6 cup, "Sundial"; syrup, "Sundial"; coffee pot, individual, "Sundial".

# "Medallion"

"Medallion" was Hall's first kitchenware line, introduced in 1932. The original issue consisted of the leftover, the teapot, the six bowl set, the casserole, and the four sizes of jugs. These were made initially in the ivory and lettuce colors. Later other colors were added. Unusual pieces include the drip coffee, the stack set, the square leftover and the juicer. The juicer in any color but lettuce is rare.

| "Medallion" | Lettuce | Ivory | Other Colors |
|---|---|---|---|
| Bowl, #2 | 2.50-3.00 | 1.50-2.00 | 3.00-3.50 |
| Bowl, #3 | 3.00-4.00 | 2.00-3.00 | 4.00-5.00 |
| Bowl, #4 | 3.00-4.00 | 2.50-3.00 | 4.00-5.00 |
| Bowl, #5 | 4.00-6.00 | 3.00-4.00 | 6.00-8.00 |
| Bowl, #6 | 7.00-9.00 | 5.00-7.00 | 8.00-10.00 |
| Casserole | 12.00-15.00 | 8.00-10.00 | 12.00-15.00 |
| Custard | 2.50-3.00 | 1.50-2.00 | 3.00-4.00 |
| Creamer | 4.00-5.00 | 2.00-3.00 | 4.00-5.00 |
| Drip coffee | 45.00-50.00 | 25.00-30.00 | 55.00-60.00 |
| Drip jar | 7.00-9.00 | 6.00-7.00 | 7.00-0.00 |
| Jug, ice lip, 4 pt. | 9.00-11.00 | 6.00-8.00 | 10.00-12.00 |
| Jug, ice lip, 5 pt. | 12.00-14.00 | 8.00-10.00 | 12.00-14.00 |
| Jug, #2 4¼", #3 5", #4 5½" | 6.00-9.00 | 4.00-7.00 | 6.00-9.00 |
| Jug, #5 6½", #6 7" | 9.00-12.00 | 8.00-10.00 | 9.00-12.00 |
| Leftover, square | 25.00-30.00 | 10.00-15.00 | 25.00-30.00 |
| Reamer | 150.00-175.00 | 175.00-200.00 | 250.00-300.00* |
| Shakers | 18.00-20.00 | 10.00-12.00 | 20.00-25.00 |
| Stack set | 35.00-40.00 | 16.00-18.00 | 28.00-30.00 |
| Sugar | 4.00-5.00 | 2.00-3.00 | 4.00-5.00 |
| Teapot | 25.00-30.00 | 25.00-30.00 | 35.00-40.00 |

*Red 350.00-400.00

**Row 1:** Leftover, square; custard; teapot. **Row 2:** Juicer; casserole; juicer. **Row 3:** Drip coffee; bowl #3; jug #5.

# "Ribbed"

"Ribbed" kitchenware was introduced in 1935 as Russetware. The line was named for the russet color of the original issue. Today, any color except Chinese red is hard-to-find. Even finding an abundance of Chinese red is difficult. The bakers, custards and ramekins came in a wide assortment of sizes as is shown in the price listing below. The 12 ounce covered onion soup (sometimes called a marmite) is found listed in a 1935 Sears' catalogue. Original prices included a set of six custard cups for $1.79; the bean pot for $1.15; and the individual onion soup for 49¢. The casserole was advertised as a five purpose casserole. It could be used as an open baker, a pie plate (the cover inverted), a two-unit baker (the casserole with the cover inverted), or as a covered baker. Russetware was heralded as "an inexpensive reproduction of expensive imported china" and was also listed by the Good Housekeeping Institute.

The two sizes of teapots, the bean pot and the covered skillet are not often seen. See page 91 for a picture of the skillet.

| "Ribbed" | Russet/Red | Other Colors |
|---|---|---|
| Baker, 8,10,12 oz. diag. rib | 4.00-5.00 | 3.00-4.00 |
| Baker, 1,1½,2,pt. diag. rib | 5.00-7.00 | 4.00-5.00 |
| Baker, 2,3, qt. diag. rib | 10.00-12.00 | 9.00-11.00 |
| Baker, 2½, 3 pt. vert. rib | 7.00-8.00 | 4.00-6.00 |
| Baker, 2, 3 qt. vert. rib | 10.00-12.00 | 9.00-11.00 |
| Bean pot | 37.00-40.00 | 28.00-30.00 |
| Bowl, 9″ salad | 16.00-18.00 | 12.00-14.00 |
| Bowl, 6¼″ | 6.00-7.00 | 5.00-6.00 |
| Bowl, 8¼″ | 7.00-9.00 | 6.00-8.00 |
| Bowl, 9½″ | 10.00-12.00 | 8.00-10.00 |
| Casserole, 8″ | 18.00-20.00 | 14.00-16.00 |
| Casserole, 9″ | 25.00-27.00 | 18.00-20.00 |
| Custard, 3½,5,7 oz | 4.00-7.00 | 3.00-6.00 |
| Onion soup, Individual | 18.00-20.00 | 12.00-14.00 |
| Ramekin, 2, 2¾ oz. | 4.00-5.00 | 3.00-3.50 |
| Ramekin, 4, 4½ oz. | 5.00-6.00 | 4.00-5.00 |
| Ramekin, 6 oz. | 5.50-6.50 | 4.00-5.00 |
| Ramekin, 4 oz. scallopped | 5.00-6.50 | 4.00-5.00 |
| Shaker, handled, ea. | 7.00-9.00 | 6.00-7.00 |
| Skillet, covered | 45.00-50.00 | 25.00-30.00 |
| Teapot, 6 cup | 45.00-50.00 | 40.00-45.00 |
| Teapot, 8 cup | 45.00-50.00 | 40.00-45.00 |

**Row 1:** Teapot, 6 cup, "Ribbed"; salad bowl, 9″, "Ribbed"; casserole, "Ribbed". **Row 2:** Pepper and salt, handled, "Ribbed"; onion soup, "Ribbed"; baker, french, "Ribbed". **Row 3:** Teapot, 6 cup, "Pert"; teapot, 6 cup, gold decorated, "Pert"; jug, $6^1/_2$″, "Pert". **Row 4:** Casserole, tab-handled; salt and pepper, "Pert".

# "Pert", Tab-handled, Straight-sided

"Pert" kitchenware was introduced in 1941. The most common colors are Chinese red/white and cadet/white. These pieces always have solid colored bodies with contrasting Hi-white handles and knobs. A "Pert" shape gold decorated teapot is shown in the photograph on page 89. These came in a variety of colors and were part of the gold decorated line.

The tab-handled and straight-sided shapes are usually found in Chinese red or cadet with contrasting Hi-white features, and are associated with the "Pert" line. Therefore, these pieces will be priced here along with "Pert".

| Kitchenware | Chinese red | Cadet |
|---|---|---|
| Bean pot, tab-handled | 30.00-32.50 | 22.00-25.00 |
| Bowl, 5¼" straight-sided | 4.00-5.00 | 4.00-5.00 |
| Bowl, 6" straight-sided | 6.00-7.00 | 5.00-6.00 |
| Bowl, 7½" straight-sided | 7.00-9.00 | 7.00-9.00 |
| Bowl, 9" straight-sided | 10.00-12.00 | 10.00-12.00 |
| Casserole, tab-handled | 18.00-20.00 | 22.00-25.00 |
| Creamer, "Pert" | 5.00-6.00 | 6.00-7.00 |
| Custard, straight-sided | 3.00-4.00 | 4.00-5.00 |
| Drip jar, tab-handled | 12.00-14.00 | 11.00-13.00 |
| Jug, 5" "Pert" | 8.00-9.00 | 8.00-9.00 |
| Jug, 6½" "Pert" | 9.00-11.00 | 9.00-11.00 |
| Jug, 7½" "Pert" | 11.00-13.00 | 11.00-13.00 |
| Shaker, "Pert", ea. | 5.00-6.00 | 4.00-5.00 |
| Sugar, "Pert" | 4.00-5.00 | 4.00-5.00 |
| Teapot, 4 cup, "Pert" | 16.00-18.00 | 14.00-16.00 |
| Teapot, 6 cup, "Pert" | 22.00-25.00 | 18.00-20.00 |

"Ribbed" Covered Skillet

Straightsided Rose White 9″ bowl; tab-handled Rose Parade casserole.

## Smart Tea Service

To you who love the beauty of smart, modern styling, and the flavor of delicious tea . . . Hall China Teapots bring double pleasure. Famous Hall Brewers are made of secret process china that will not stain . . . and their gleaming gold decorations glisten on glaze that will not craze! If you cannot obtain the style you prefer please remember that much of our production of chinaware is for our fighting forces. The Hall China Company — World's Largest Manufacturer of Decorated Teapots and Cooking China.

*Teapots of superior quality china . . .*

by *Hall*

* * * SOLD BY ALL LEADING DEALERS * *

# "Radiance"

Introduced in 1933, "Radiance" was Hall's second kitchenware line. "Radiance" may be found in a variety of colors, but Chinese red is the most common and the most desirable to collectors. The easiest pieces to find are the mixing bowls and the medium-size jugs. However the lids to the jugs are not always easy to locate. The most difficult pieces to find are the condiment jar and the drip coffee. The cereal set which includes four canisters and two shakers is very desirable and has skyrocketed in price. The cereal set was made in a variety of colors starting in 1938. Many pieces of the "Radiance" shape will be found in the various decal lines.

| "Radiance" | Red/Cobalt | Ivory | Other Colors |
|---|---|---|---|
| Bowl, 3½" #1 | 3.00-4.00 | 2.00-3.00 | 2.50-3.00 |
| Bowl, 5¼" #2 | 4.00-5.00 | 2.50-3.00 | 4.00-5.00 |
| Bowl, 6" #3 | 5.00-6.00 | 3.00-3.50 | 4.00-5.00 |
| Bowl, 7½" #4 | 6.00-8.00 | 4.00-5.00 | 5.00-7.00 |
| Bowl, 9" #5 | 10.00-12.00 | 5.00-6.00 | 7.00-9.00 |
| Bowl, 10" #6 | 15.00-17.00 | 6.00-8.00 | 10.00-12.00 |
| Canister, 2 qt. | 40.00-45.00 | 18.00-20.00 | 35.00-40.00 |
| Casserole | 25.00-30.00 | 10.00-12.00 | 18.00-20.00 |
| Condiment jar | 45.00-50.00 | 18.00-20.00 | 35.00-37.00 |
| Drip coffee | 75.00-80.00 | 25.00-30.00 | 65.00-70.00 |
| Drip jar | 15.00-17.00 | 7.00-9.00 | 10.00-12.00 |
| *Jug, 3¼" #1; 4¼" #2 | 25.00-27.00 | 8.00-10.00 | 16.00-18.00 |
| *Jug, 4¾" #3; 5¼" #4 | 28.00-30.00 | 10.00-12.00 | 18.00-20.00 |
| *Jug, 6¼" #5; 6¾" #6 | 30.00-35.00 | 12.00-14.00 | 20.00-25.00 |
| Shaker, 14 oz. | 12.00-14.00 | 8.00-10.00 | 10.00-12.00 |
| Stack set | 35.00-40.00 | 10.00-12.00 | 28.00-32.00 |
| Teapot, 6 cup | 45.00-50.00 | 25.00-30.00 | 37.00-40.00 |

*With lid

**Row 1:** Canister, sugar; canister, flour; canister, tea; canister, coffee. **Row 2:** Salt and pepper; jug and cover; bowl, size #2; salt and pepper. **Row 3:** Canister, sugar; canister, flour; canister, tea; canister, coffee.

# Rose White and Rose Parade

Rose White and Rose Parade were kitchenware lines introduced in the 1940's which utilized the "Pert", tab-handled and straight-sided shapes. The Rose White body was Hi-white, trimmed in silver, and decorated with a pink floral decal. The Rose Parade pieces had a cadet body with contrasting Hi-white knobs or handles. The decoration used was either a red or a blue rose decal. The blue rose pieces are not found as frequently as the red. The popularity of Rose Parade among collectors has increased significantly in the last few years.

| Kitchenware | Rose White | Rose Parade |
|---|---|---|
| Baker, french | 10.00-14.00 | 14.00-16.00 |
| Bean pot, tab-handled | 32.00-35.00 | 37.00-40.00 |
| Bowl, 9″ salad | 10.00-12.00 | 12.00-14.00 |
| Bowl, 6″ straight-sided #3 | 7.00-9.00 | 10.00-11.00 |
| Bowl, 7½″ straight-sided #4 | 8.00-10.00 | 12.00-14.00 |
| Bowl, 9″ straight-sided #5 | 12.00-14.00 | 14.00-15.00 |
| Casserole, tab-handled | 22.00-25.00 | 18.00-20.00 |
| Creamer, "Pert" | 5.50-6.50 | 6.00-8.00 |
| Custard, straight-sided | 4.00-5.00 | 4.00-5.00 |
| Drip jar, tab-handled | 14.00-15.00 | 16.00-18.00 |
| Jug, 5″ "Pert" | 12.00-14.00 | 14.00-15.00 |
| Jug, 6½″ "Pert" | 16.00-18.00 | 17.00-18.00 |
| Jug, 7½″ "Pert" | 20.00-22.00 | 22.00-25.00 |
| Shaker, "Pert", ea. | 5.00-6.00 | 6.00-7.00 |
| Sugar, "Pert" | 5.50-6.50 | 6.00-8.00 |
| Teapot, 4 cup, "Pert" | 16.00-18.00 | 18.00-20.00 |
| Teapot, 6 cup, "Pert" | 20.00-22.00 | 22.00-24.00 |

**Row 1:** Bean pot, tab-handled, Rose White; jug, 6¹/₂″ "Pert", Rose White; salt and pepper, "Pert," Rose White. **Row 2:** Bean pot, tab-handled, Rose Parade; casserole, tab-handled, Rose Parade; salt and pepper, "Pert", Rose Parade. **Row 3:** Jug, 7¹/₂″, "Pert", Rose Parade; jug, 6¹/₂″, "Pert", Rose Parade; teapot, "Pert", Rose Parade; drip jar, tab-handled, Rose Parade. **Row 4:** Bowl, "Thick Rim", Royal Rose; ball jug #3, Royal Rose.

# Royal Rose and Morning Glory

Royal Rose kitchenware has a cadet body with contrasting Hi-white features. The decal used was the same pink rose decal that was used on Rose White. Many people often confuse this pattern with Rose Parade, but the Royal Rose pieces are accented with silver trim and the shapes are different from those used in the Rose Parade line.

Morning Glory is a small line produced in the forties for Jewel Tea to co-ordinate with their Wildwood pattern dinnerware. These pieces feature a cadet body with contrasting Hi-white features and a morning glory decal.

| Kitchenware | Royal Rose | Morning Glory |
|---|---|---|
| Ball jug#3 | 25.00-30.00 | |
| Bowl, 6" "Thick Rim" | 9.00-11.00 | |
| Bowl, 7½" "Thick Rim" | 12.00-15.00 | |
| Bowl, 8½" "Thick Rim" | 14.00-16.00 | |
| Bowl, 6" straight-sided | | 7.00-8.00 |
| Bowl, 7½" straight-sided | | 10.00-12.00 |
| Bowl, 9" straight-sided | | 14.00-16.00 |
| Casserole, "Thick Rim" | 20.00-22.00 | |
| Custard, straight-sided | | 4.00-5.00 |
| Drip coffee, all-china | | 60.00-65.00 |
| Drip jar, "Thick Rim" | 16.00-18.00 | |
| Shaker, handled, ea. | 7.00-8.00 | |
| Teapot, Aladdin | | 40.00-45.00 |
| Teapot, french | 30.00-32.00 | |

**Row 1:** Bowl, 8¹/₂″ "Thick Rim", Royal Rose; bowl, 7¹/₂″ "Thick Rim", Royal Rose; bowl, ₅″, "Thick Rim", Royal Rose. **Row 2:** Pepper, handled, Royal Rose; drip jar, "Thick Rim", Royal Rose; salt, handled, Royal Rose. **Row 3:** Teapot, French, Royal Rose; casserole, "Thick Rim", Royal Rose. **Row 4:** Bowl, straightsided, Morning Glory; all-china drip coffee, Morning Glory; teapot, Aladdin, Morning Glory.

# Blue Blossom

Blue Blossom is a scarcely found decal kitchenware line. The line was introduced in 1939 and was only produced for a few years. There is little information available on this line. We have listed the known pieces, but a lot of new shapes with this decal have been discovered recently, and more are sure to be found.

| Blue Blossom | Price |
|---|---|
| Ball jug #1 | 45.00-50.00 |
| Ball jug #2 | 47.00-52.00 |
| Ball jug#3 | 45.00-50.00 |
| Batter jug, "Sundial" | 85.00-100.00 |
| Bean pot, New England #4 | 125.00-150.00 |
| Bowl, 6″ "Thick Rim" | 27.00-32.00 |
| Bowl, 7½″ "Thick Rim" | 25.00-30.00 |
| Bowl, 8½″ "Thick Rim" | 27.00-32.00 |
| Casserole, "Thick Rim" | 35.00-40.00 |
| Casserole, "Sundial" #1 | 30.00-32.00 |
| Casserole, "Sundial" #4 | 28.00-30.00 |
| Coffee server, "Sundial" | 20.00-25.00 |
| Cookie jar, "Five Band" | 85.00-100.00 |
| Cookie jar, "Sundial" | 150.00-200.00 |
| Creamer, morning | 20.00-22.00 |
| Custard, "Thick Rim" | 12.00-14.00 |
| Drip, #1188 open | 25.00-30.00 |
| Jug, loop handle | 45.00-50.00 |
| Leftover, loop handle | 50.00-60.00 |
| Shaker, "Five Band", ea. | 12.50-15.00 |
| Shaker, handled, ea. | 14.00-16.00 |
| Sugar and lid, morning | 28.00-32.00 |
| Syrup, "Sundial" | 65.00-75.00 |
| Teapot, morning | 85.00-100.00 |
| Teapot, "Sundial" | 95.00-125.00 |
| Teapot, Streamline | 95.00-125.00 |

**Row 1:** Cookie jar, "Five Band"; teapot, "Sundial"; cookie jar, "Sundial". **Row 2:** Teapot, morning; sugar and creamer, morning; salt and pepper, handled. **Row 3:** Syrup, "Sundial"; casserole, "Thick Rim"; ball jug #1. **Row 4:** Batter jug, "Sundial"; bowl, $8^1/_2''$ "Thick Rim".

# Blue Garden

Blue Garden is another cobalt kitchenware line with a floral decal which was introduced in the late 1930's. All pieces are hard to find with the exception of the "Sundial" #4 casserole, which is abundant. Not nearly as many pieces of Blue Garden appear to be available as there are in Blue Blossom. Therefore, there is less collector interest in this pattern and prices are not as high.

| Blue Garden | Price |
|---|---|
| Batter jug, "Sundial" | 85.00-100.00 |
| Butter, 1# "Zephyr" Style | 150.00-200.00 |
| Casserole, "Sundial"#4 | 22.00-25.00 |
| Creamer, morning | 18.00-20.00 |
| Shaker, handled, ea. | 12.00-14.00 |
| Sugar and lid, morning | 25.00-27.00 |
| Syrup, "Sundial" | 45.00-55.00 |
| Teapot, morning | 60.00-70.00 |
| Teapot, New York | 85.00-100.00 |

**Row 1:** Teapot, Streamline; jug, loop handle. **Row 2:** Shakers, "Five Band"; casserole, "Sundial #1"; custard, "Thick Rim". **Row 3:** Leftover, loop handle; shakers, handled; sugar and creamer, morning . **Row 4:** Batter jug, "Sundial"; casserole, "Sundial" #4; syrup, "Sundial".

# Cactus, Clover, Meadow Flower, Fantasy, Acacia

Cactus was introduced in 1937 and was offered for several years. All pieces are hard-to-find with the exception of the "Viking" Drip-o-lator coffee pot and the "Five-Band" syrup. Notice the french style teapot in the photograph with the rare cactus decal.

Clover is a decal which is scarcely found. Some of the more desirable pieces with this decal are the windshield teapot and the Ziesel cookie jar.

Meadow Flower is a hard-to-find decal which has appeared on a limited number of Hall pieces. Fantasy is another scarce decal. The casseroles and shakers are the only pieces turning up with any frequency.

Acacia decals are found most frequently on the "Radiance" jugs. Other pieces of Acacia are not often seen. Taylor-Smith and Taylor also used this decal on one of their dinnerware lines. To date, no Hall dinnerware has been found in any of these patterns.

| Cactus | Price |
|---|---|
| Ball jug #3 | 30.00-32.00 |
| Batter bowl, "Five Band" | 27.00-30.00 |
| Casserole, "Five Band" | 35.00-37.00 |
| Coffee pot, "Five Band" | 22.00-25.00 |
| Coffee pot, "Viking" | 25.00-27.00 |
| Cookie jar, "Five Band" | 40.00-45.00 |
| Jug, 1½ pt., "Five Band" | 40.00-45.00 |
| Jug, 2 qt., "Five Band" | 45.00-50.00 |
| Shakers, handled ea. | 12.00-14.00 |
| Stack set, "Radiance" | 45.00-55.00 |
| Syrup, "Five Band" | 27.00-30.00 |
| Teapot, French | 45.00-55.00 |

| Acacia | Price |
|---|---|
| Bean pot, New England #4 | 75.00-80.00 |
| Casserole, "Medallion" | 32.00-35.00 |
| Casserole, "Radiance" | 30.00-32.00 |
| Custard, "Radiance" | 4.50-5.50 |
| Jug and cover, "Radiance" #2 | 40.00-45.00 |
| Jug and cover, "Radiance" #3 | 45.00-55.00 |
| Marmite and cover | 20.00-22.00 |
| Shakers, handled, ea. | 14.00-16.00 |

| Clover | Price |
|---|---|
| Casserole, "Radiance" | 25.00-30.00 |
| Cookie jar, Ziesel style | 40.00-45.00 |
| Shakers, handled, ea. | 12.00-15.00 |
| Teapot, windshield | 45.00-50.00 |

| Fantasy | Price |
|---|---|
| Ball jug # 3 | 45.00-55.00 |
| Bean pot, New England # 4 | 60.00-65.00 |
| Batter jug, "Sundial" | 95.00-110.00 |
| Casserole, "Thick Rim" | 32.00-37.00 |
| Casserole, "Sundial" | 32.00-35.00 |
| Shakers, handled, ea. | 15.00-18.00 |

| Meadow Flower | Price |
|---|---|
| Ball jug #3 | 35.00-40.00 |
| Bean pot, New England #4 | 65.00-75.00 |
| Casserole, "Radiance" | 35.00-40.00 |
| Cookie jar, "Five Band" | 65.00-70.00 |

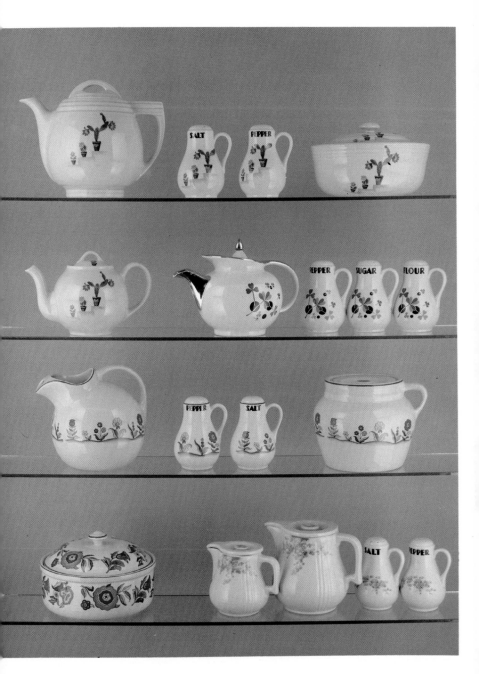

**Row 1:** Coffee pot, "Viking", Cactus; shakers, handled, Cactus; casserole, "Five Band", Cactus. **Row 2:** Teapot, French, Cactus; teapot, Windshield, Clover; shakers, handled, Clover. **Row 3:** Ball jug #3, Meadow Flower; shakers, handled, Meadow Flower; bean pot, New England #4, Meadow Flower. **Row 4:** Casserole, "Thick Rim", Fantasy; jug, "Radiance" #2, Acacia; jug "Radiance" #4, Acacia; shakers, handled, Acacia.

# #488 and Shaggy Tulip

The #488 line was introduced in the early thirties and was offered until the end of the decade. We seem to find more pieces of #488 available in eastern Pennsylvania than anywhere else. However, this pattern is not easy to find and there are probably many more pieces to still be discovered. No Hall dinnerware has been seen in this pattern.

Shaggy Tulip is another decal about which very little is known. The pattern probably dates from the mid-thirties to the mid-forties. The only piece of this pattern which turns up frequently is the all-china drip coffee. A rolling pin, pie lifter, spoon, and fork have been found in this pattern. These pieces are not Hall and were probably made by Harker.

| Item | #488 | Shaggy Tulip |
|---|---|---|
| Bean pot, New England (#3,#4,#5) | 45.00-55.00 | |
| Bowl, "Radiance" #3 | 8.00-10.00 | |
| Bowl, "Radiance" #4 | 10.00-12.00 | |
| Bowl, "Radiance" #5 | 14.00-16.00 | |
| Casserole, "Thick Rim" | 30.00-32.00 | |
| Casserole, "Radiance" | 22.00-27.00 | |
| Condiment Jar, "Radiance" | 85.00-95.00 | |
| Custard, "Radiance" | 5.00-6.00 | |
| Drip Coffee | | 60.00-65.00 |
| Drip Coffee, "Radiance" | 120.00-130.00 | |
| Drip jar, "Radiance" | 18.00-20.00 | |
| Drip, #1188 open | 25.00-30.00 | |
| Jug, "Medallion", ice lip | 37.00-42.00 | |
| *Jug, "Radiance" (#2,#3) | 25.00-27.00 | 25.00-30.00 |
| *Jug, "Radiance" (#4,#5,#6) | 30.00-35.00 | |
| Pretzel jar | | 80.00-90.00 |
| Refrigerator jar, square | 45.00-55.00 | |
| Shakers, handled, ea. | 9.00-11.00 | 8.00-10.00 |
| Shakers, "Novelty" | 12.00-14.00 | 12.00-14.00 |
| Shirred egg dish | 22.00-25.00 | |
| Stack set, "Radiance" | 60.00-65.00 | 55.00-60.00 |
| Teapot, "Radiance" | 85.00-95.00 | 85.00-95.00 |

*With lids, add 40%

Drip coffee, all-china Shaggy Tulip; shakers, "Novelty", Shaggy Tulip; shakers, handled, Shaggy Tulip.

Left to right: #488 "Radiance" casserole; #488 "Radiance" stack set; #488 "Novelty" shakers; #488 shirred egg dish; Shaggy Tulip pretzel jar.

**Row 1:** Jug and cover, "Radiance"; jug, "Radiance"; salt, handled; drip, #1188 open; pepper and sugar, handled. **Row 2:** Bowl set, "Radiance" bean pot, New England #4.

# Miscellaneous Kitchenware

The Radiant Ware bowls were produced for the Jewel Tea Company during the early forties. The complete set consists of four bowls. Each size bowl was made in a different color--#1 green, #2 yellow, #3 blue, #4 red.

The red dots on eggshell white are unusual. A few more pieces have been seen and more are sure to turn up. The presence of the sugar shaker means this set exists as a four piece set.

The Plum Pudding bowls exist in a variety of sizes and patterns. Some of these bowls have advertising stamped on the reverse side. A complete list of the sizes available is listed below. Not every decal was available in all the sizes.

The yellow pieces with the gold decoration were part of a bakeware line designed by J. Palin Thorley. There are more pieces to this line than those pictured.

| Radiant Ware Bowls | Price |
|---|---|
| #1 green | 4.00-6.00 |
| #2 yellow | 6.00-7.50 |
| #4 blue | 8.00-10.00 |
| #4 red | 14.00-16.00 |

| Plum Pudding Bowls | Price |
|---|---|
| #1, 4½" | 3.00-4.00 |
| #2, 5" | 4.00-5.00 |
| #3, 6" | 6.00-7.00 |
| #4, 6½" | 7.00-8.00 |
| #5, 7½" | 7.00-9.00 |
| #6, 9" | 9.00-10.00 |
| #7, 11" | 10.00-12.00 |
| #8, 13" | 14.00-16.00 |

| Red Dot on Eggshell White | Price |
|---|---|
| Bowl, 6" | 7.00-8.00 |
| Bowl, 7½" | 9.00-11.00 |
| Bowl, 9" | 11.00-13.00 |
| Casserole, oval | 16.00-18.00 |
| Casserole, round | 16.00-18.00 |
| Shakers, handled, ea. | 7.00-9.00 |

| Thorley Bakeware | Price |
|---|---|
| Bowl, 6" | 4.00-5.00 |
| Bowl 7½" | 5.00-7.00 |
| Bowl, 9" | 7.00-9.00 |
| Casserole, round | 10.00-12.00 |
| Cookie jar | 20.00-25.00 |

| Miscellaneous | Price |
|---|---|
| Baker, round | 4.00-6.00 |
| Shakers, Red dot on ivory, ea. | 7.00-9.00 |

**Row 1:** Radiant Ware bowl; Radiant Ware bowl; Red Dot on Eggshell white oval casserole.
**Row 2:** Bowl, 9″ Red Dot; bowl, 7$^1/_2$″ Red Dot; bowl, 6″ Red Dot; sugar, handled, Red Dot. **Row 3:** Set Plum Pudding bowls, Holly design; shakers, handled. **Row 4:** Casserole, round, Thorley; baker, round; baker, round. **Row 5:** Bowl, 9″ Thorley; bowl, 7$^1/_2$″ Thorley; owl, 6″ Thorley.

# Gold Label and Other Kitchenware

The Gold Label line was introduced in the fifties. This line consisted of teapots chosen from the old Gold Decorated line and the following matching accessory pieces; a 9″ salad bowl, a "Radiance" jug, a "Terrace" coffee pot, a Zeisel cookie jar, a #101 round casserole, and the "Thick Rim" 3-piece bowl set. Each design is usually only found in one color, although some of the teapots were made in several colors. Also, the teapot selected was usually the six cup size, but some other size Gold Label teapots are found. The Gold Label teapots have the letters "GL" following the gold code number on the base.

| Teapot | Primary Color | Design | Price |
|---|---|---|---|
| Aladdin | Marine | Swag | 32.00-35.00 |
| Albany | Mahogany | Reflection | 40.00-45.00 |
| Baltimore | Maroon | Nova | 32.00-35.00 |
| Boston | Dresden | Fleur-de-lis | 30.00-32.00 |
| French | Blue turquoise | Daisy | 25.00-28.00 |
| Hollywood | Pink | Grid | 25.00-27.00 |
| Hook Cover | Cadet | Star | 16.00-18.00 |
| Los Angeles | Monterrey | Medallion | 25.00-28.00 |
| New York | Canary | Flower | 22.00-25.00 |
| Parade | Canary | Squiggle | 18.00-20.00 |
| Philadelphia | Pink | Basket | 18.00-20.00 |
| Windshield | Camellia | Dot | 18.00-20.00 |

| Accessory Pieces | Price |
|---|---|
| "Thick Rim" bowl set | 30.00-35.00 |
| Bowl, 9″ salad | 10.00-12.00 |
| Casserole, #101 | 25.00-27.00 |
| Coffee pot, "Terrace" | 22.00-27.00 |
| Cookie jar, Zeisel | 18.00-20.00 |
| Jug, "Radiance" | 9.00-11.00 |

**Row 1:** Coffee pot, "Terrace", squiggle design; cookie jar, Zeisel, squiggle design; baker, French, squiggle design. **Row 2:** Bowl, 9″ salad, squiggle design; cookie jar, Zeisel, medallion design; teapot, Los Angeles, medallion design. **Row 3:** Cookie jar, Zeisel, star design; cookie jar, Zeisel, dot design; teapot, Philadelphia, basket design. **Row 4:** Ball jug, floral design; bean pot, New England #4, ivory/red stripe; bean pot, New England #4, brown/yellow lid.

Genuine Hall china. Choice of 3 colors. At your grocer's. Supply limited. Hurry!

*Get this beautiful*

# ICED TEA PITCHER

ONLY **89¢** (**$2.00 VALUE**)
with purchase of
McCormick Tea or Tea Bags
(This offer not available in certain areas.)

## McCORMICK TEA

It's the *Magic Blend* of the choicest tea leaves grown
...created by the world's foremost flavor experts.

**Mc TEA BAGS McCORMICK**

For years, the wonderful flavor of McCormick Tea has been protected in *foil-lined tea bag cartons*.

**Mc** McCORMICK
ONE FAMOUS EMBLEM—TWO GREAT BRANDS
**McCORMICK** and
Schilling

THE HOUSE OF McCORMICK

# Part III: Refrigerator Ware

With the advent of the modern refrigerator in the late 1930's, the need for new cold storage accessories developed. Many china companies produced wares which were sold for this purpose. However, a few companies also produced items which were offered for sale with the new refrigerator by the dealer. In addition to items for retail sale, Hall produced various articles for Westinghouse, General Electric, Sears, and Hotpoint. Hall also produced refrigerator items to be used as premiums for companies such as McCormick Tea. The accompanying reprint is an example of one such premium.

Three basic items were included in the Hall refrigerator line. They included water bottles or water servers, leftovers, and butters.

The water containers were covered pieces intended to be placed in the refrigerator for water storage. Closure was effected with either a cork-encased china stopper or with a china lid. Leftovers were deep dishes with a shallow or flat china lid. Butters had a flat bottom and a deep lid.

The collection of Hall refrigerator ware has been neglected until recently. Now many people who have failed to realize the quality and durability of these pieces are beginning to buy these useful items. These bargain-priced items are again seeing service in the modern refrigerator.

"Zephyr" water bottles.

# Westinghouse

"Hercules" was offered as "Peasant Ware" by Westinghouse in 1940 and 1941. A set consisted of a rectangular butter, a water server and two leftovers.

"General" was offered in 1939 as an accessory to Westinghouse refrigerators. Sets consisted of a water server, two leftovers, and a butter. The most common color for the water server is delphinium. The butter and leftovers are usually garden, sunset, delphinium, or canary.

"Phoenix" was the earliest line of Hall refrigerator ware used by Westinghouse. This line was introduced in 1938 and consisted of a water server, a leftover and a butter. The most commonly found color is delphinium, but other colors do exist.

The "Adonis" line in blue and daffodil was offered by Westinghouse in 1952. A set consisted of a water server, four small round leftovers, and two rectangular leftovers. Ovenware sets were also offered at the same time. These pieces are shown on the next page. Each line consisted of three pieces--two covered roasters and one open roaster. The "Ridged" line was made in canary and the "Plain" line came in delphinium.

| Refrigerator Ware | "Hercules" | "General" | Phoenix | Adonis |
|---|---|---|---|---|
| Butter | 10.00-12.00 | 10.00-12.00 | 9.00-11.00 | |
| Leftover, rect. | 6.00-7.00 | 7.00-8.00 | 6.50-7.50 | 6.00-7.00 |
| Leftover, round | | | | 5.00-6.00 |
| Water server | 40.00-45.00 | 20.00-25.00 | 20.00-22.00 | 14.00-16.00 |
| **Bakeware** | **"Ridged"** | **"Plain"** | | |
| Casserole, Covered | 10.00-12.00 | 10.00-12.00 | | |
| Casserole, open | 5.00-6.00 | 5.00-6.00 | | |

**Row 1:** Water server, "Hercules"; water server, "Hercules"; leftover, "Hercules"; butter, "Hercules". **Row 2:** Leftover, "General"; butter, "General"; water server, "General". **Row 3:** Water server, "Phoenix"; leftover, "Phoenix"; butter, "Phoenix". **Row 4:** Leftover, rectangular, "Adonis"; water server, "Adonis"; leftover, small round, "Adonis".

# Montgomery Ward, Hotpoint, Sears, General Electric

A line consisting of a least eight pieces was made for Montgomery Ward in the early forties. Most of the pieces were in the delphinium color, but all of the pieces seem to also exist in the seldom-seen mid-white color. There are two styles of rectangular leftover. The larger one with the strange lid is unusual. Another piece which does not turn up very often is a covered bowl with a large raised, scalloped handle. The bowl also has matching scallops around the base. There are also three sizes of covered bowls with raised, elongated handles, a rectangular butter, and a water server.

| Refrigerator Ware | Price | Refrigerator Ware | Price |
|---|---|---|---|
| Bowl, sm. covered | 10.00-12.00 | Butter | 20.00-22.00 |
| Bowl, med.covered | 12.00-14.00 | Leftover,rect. | 8.00-10.00 |
| Bowl, lg. covered | 14.00-16.00 | Leftover, lg. rect. | 18.00-20.00 |
| Bowl, knob handle | 12.00-14.00 | Water server | 20.00-22.00 |

Hall produced a colorful refrigerator line for Hotpoint. Included were a water server, three round leftovers, five square leftovers, and a rectangular leftover. The water server, square leftovers, and the rectangular leftover are not easy-to-find. The round leftovers are available, but usually at a high price. For some reason the presence of the Hotpoint insignia on the pieces mysteriously raises their value. Remember, the water server should have a cork-encased stopper and the leftovers are not complete without lids.

| Refrigerator Ware | Price | Refrigerator Ware | Price |
|---|---|---|---|
| Leftover, rect. | 10.00-12.00 | Leftover, 4¾″ sq. | 8.00-10.00 |
| Leftover, 6¾″ round | 8.00-10.00 | Leftover, 5¾″ sq. | 10.00-12.00 |
| Leftover, 7¾″ round | 12.00-14.00 | Leftover, 6¾″ sq. | 16.00-18.00 |
| Leftover, 8¾″ round | 16.00-18.00 | Leftover, 8½″ sq. | 20.00-22.00 |
| Leftover, 4″ sq. | 7.00-9.00 | Water server | 25.00-27.00 |

Hall made one piece of refrigerator ware for Sears. This was a 3-part leftover in cadet and Hi-white. The center piece was solid cadet and the end sections had cadet bases with Hi-white lids.

Sears leftover, 3-part    25.00-27.00

Hall modified its Westinghouse "Adonis" line for use with General Electric refrigerators. The GE logo was used on the lids and the new colors used were addison and daffodil. Two new pieces were added--a handled casserole and a large round leftover.

| General Electric | Price | General Electric | Price |
|---|---|---|---|
| Casserole | 12.00-14.00 | Leftover, lg. round | 9.00-11.00 |
| Leftover, rect. | 7.00-8.00 | Water server | 12.00-14.00 |
| Leftover, sm. round | 3.00-4.00 | | |

**Row 1:** Roaster, covered, "Ridged", Westinghouse; roaster, open, "Ridged", Westinghouse; roaster, covered, "Plain", Westinghouse. **Row 2:** Leftover, rectangular, Montgomery Ward; bowl, covered, Montgomery Ward; water server, Montgomery Ward; leftover, rectangular, Montgomery Ward. **Row 3:** Water server, Hotpoint; leftover, $8^1/_2''$ square, Hotpoint; leftover, $6^3/_4''$ round, Hotpoint. **Row 4:** Leftover, 3-section, Sears. **Row 5:** Water server, General Electric; casserole, General Electric; leftover, rectangular, General Electric.

# Miscellaneous Refrigerator Ware

Hall made some refrigerator ware under their own logo for retail sale. Among these items were the Plaza water server, the "Nora" water server, and the "Zephyr" line.

The Plaza water server comes with a cork-enclosed china stopper and was produced from the thirties to the sixties. Even with this long period of production, the Plaza server is not easy to find today. Even fewer are found complete with their china stoppers.

The "Zephyr" line consists of two sizes of stoppered water bottles, a rectangular leftover, and a one-pound butter. This line dates from the latter thirties and appears to have only been made in Chinese red. The two size water bottles are shown on page 111.

The "Nora" water servers came with and without lids. They were a covered water server available in Hall's general line and also were premium item for McCormick Tea in their lidless form. See the reprint from a 1955 magazine at the beginning of this section.

The loop handle jug was introduced in the thirties. It is found in a variety of colors and was used in several decal lines. The doughnut jug is from the late thirties and is found in two sizes and a variety of colors. This jug does not appear to have been used in any of the decal lines. The larger-size jug is easier to find than the smaller one.

Ball jugs were introduced in 1938 and came in four sizes. The #3 ball jug is probably the most widely used piece Hall produced. It can be found in almost any Hall color and even has been found with some of the rarest decals, including the cactus decal in the picture.

| Refrigerator Ware | Price | Refrigerator Ware | Price |
|---|---|---|---|
| Ball jug #1, 1½ pt. | 18.00-20.00 | "Zephyr" water bottle (2 sizes) | 37.00-42.00 |
| Ball jug #2, 2½ pt. | 18.00-20.00 | Doughnut jug, small | 20.00-22.00 |
| Ball jug #3, 2 qt. | 12.00-14.00 | Doughnut jug, lg. | 22.00-25.00 |
| Ball jug #4, 5 pt. | 20.00-22.00 | Loop handle jug | 14.00-16.00 |
| "Zephyr" butter | 55.00-60.00 | "Nora" water server | 10.00-12.00 |
| "Zephyr" leftover | 32.00-37.00 | Plaza waterserver | 32.00-37.00 |

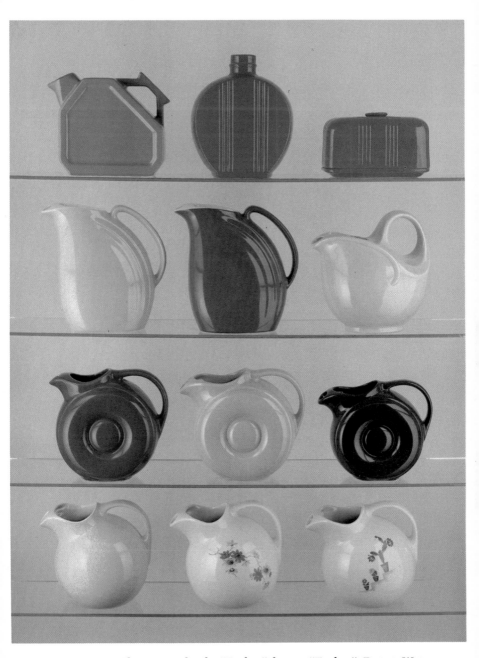

**Row 1:** Water server, Plaza; water bottle, "Zephyr"; butter, "Zephyr". **Row 2:** Water server, "Nora"; water server, "Nora"; jug, loop handle. **Row 3:** Large jug, Doughnut; large jug, Doughtnut; small jug, Doughnut. **Row 4:** Ball jug #3; ball jug #3; ball jug #3, Cactus decal.

AIRFLOW TEAPOT

## Decorated With Gold!

The lovely Airflow brewer, an exclusive Hall China design, is beautifully shaped, richly colored, and decorated with gleaming gold! Like all genuine Hall Teapots, it will not stain or absorb because it is made of secret process china that keeps sweet and clean. If your dealer does not have the exact shape or color you prefer please remember that much of our production of chinaware is for our fighting forces.

THE HALL CHINA COMPANY...World's Largest Manufacturer of Decorated Teapots and Cooking China

*Hall* **Teapots** OF SUPERIOR QUALITY CHINA

## Beauty and Utility United!

The Aladdin Teapot brings pleasure to all who love the golden beverage. It is a lovely, traditional design, enriched with genuine gold decoration. And, its use assures perfect tea every time, for it is made of secret process china that will never craze, stain, or absorb.

The Hall China Company—World's Largest Manufacturer of Decorated Teapots and Cooking China.

*Hall* **Teapots** OF SUPERIOR QUALITY CHINA

*Sold by All Leading Dealers*

## PREFERRED for Perfect Tea

This lovely French shape is decorated with gleaming gold that glistens on a colorful glaze that will never craze. Like all genuine Hall Teapots, it is made of secret process china that will not stain or absorb. Use it ... for perfect tea, graciously served. That's why Hall Teapots are preferred!

**The Hall China Company**
World's Largest Manufacturer of Decorated Teapots and Cooking China

*Hall* **Teapots** OF SUPERIOR QUALITY CHINA

*Sold by All Leading Dealers*

THE MODERNE

## Charming TEA SERVICE

Hall China Gold Decorated Teapots appeal irresistibly to all who know good tea, and appreciate lovely chinaware. Made of secret process china ... they brew tea that is deliciously delicate and fresh in flavor. If you cannot obtain the Hall teapot design you prefer, please remember that the needs of our fighting forces have first call. The Hall China Company ... World's Largest Manufacturer of Decorated Teapots and Cooking China.

*Hall* **Teapots** OF SUPERIOR QUALITY CHINA

SOLD BY ALL LEADING DEALERS

# Part IV: Teapots and Coffee Pots

The first Hall teapots were part of the institutional line. The early colors were stock brown, stock green and white. In 1920 the Boston, New York, and French shapes were selected for a store promotion. These teapots were decorated with gold and Hall's Gold Decorated Teapot line was born. The line was very successful. Over the next few decades, new shapes were added. These were combined with a rainbow of new colors. The public acceptance of these new shapes and colors soon made Hall the leading producer of teapots in the world.

Most of Hall's teapots and colors were used in the Gold Decorated line. The backstamp will include a gold code number which was used for reordering purposes. The Chinese red color was not included in the Gold Decorated line. These teapots were part of the kitchenware line. They always bear the "HALL'S SUPERIOR QUALITY KITCHENWARE" mark. Although the syle of gold decoration soon became standard on each shape teapot, some experimentation in the early years has resulted in some different gold designs on some of the older teapots.

In the early 1940's Hall introduced another line of teapots which have become known as the Victorian line. This line included six teapots, each produced in a single color. A few years later gold decoration was added in an attempt to increase sales. However the line was never very popular and was discontinued by the end of the decade.

Also in the forties, another series of teapots was designed by J. Palin Thorley. Although we only know of five, there were probably six teapots in this series. Most of these teapots were only made in a single color, but their decoration was more gaudy than the decoration of the Victorian line. Decorations included decals, rhinestones, and gold. More than one type of decoration was sometimes used on the same shape teapot. This line was discontinued by the mid-fifties.

In the late fifties, Hall brought out a new line of teapots called Gold Label. These teapots were very gaudy--almost covered with gold. The styles of teapots were selected from among those used earlier. No new shapes were introduced. This new line of teapots was sold along with other matching kitchenware accessories. The gold code number on the bottom of these teapots will be followed by the letters "GL."

Today there is serious collector interest in Hall teapots. The most desirable teapots are the hard-to-find novelty teapots. These have been known to command a premium price when an avid collector has crossed paths with a knowledgeable seller.

Hall produced many different style coffee pots. Many of these pots were used in the decal lines and will be identified there. However some were sold to other companies like Enterprise, Tricolator, and Westinghouse. These companies then added the metal parts and marketed the finished product. Some, but not all, of these coffee pots will bear the Hall mark.

To help with identification, the coffee pots and teapots in the following photographs will have both their shape name and color name. In some cases recognition of the colors may still be difficult, since some colors do not print exactly the shade they should.

# Novelty Teapots

The automobile is a six cup novelty teapot introduced in 1938. It may be found in solid colors and is also sometimes seen with either gold or silver trim. These teapots are highly collectible, hard-to-find, and very high-priced.

The basket is an unusual-looking six cup teapot which was first made in 1938. It is most commonly found in canary. Other colors including Chinese red and marine are seen less frequently.

The basketball also made its appearance in 1938. This is a very striking six cup novelty teapot. This teapot is probably the second most difficult to find of the novelty teapots. The red basketball in the picture has the Hall Superior Quality Kitchenware mark on the bottom.

The birdcage, another six cup novelty teapot, was introduced in 1939. This is an elusive teapot which is still being sought after by some veteran collectors. The gold or silver decorated varieties are particularly striking.

The doughnut teapot, which first appeared in 1938, is most commonly found in the ivory color with the Orange Poppy decal. The most commonly found solid color is Chinese red.

The football seems to be the least common of the novelty teapots. There are two other novelty type teapots turning up less frequently, but these two probably were never in regular production. One--the "bowling ball"--is pictured on page 143 and seems to be found most frequently in Kentucky. The second--a very unusual gold-decorated teapot--has just been discovered. We are calling this teapot, pictured on page 145, "the Philbe." This may have been an experimental teapot which was never released.

| Teapot | Introduced | Red/Cobalt | Other Colors | Gold/Silver-Decorated |
|--------|-----------|-----------|-------------|------------------------|
| Automobile | 1938 | 300.00-350.00 | 275.00-325.00 | 350.00-375.00 |
| Basket | 1938 | 125.00-140.00 | *60.00-70.00 | add 10% |
| Basketball | 1938 | 185.00-200.00 | 175.00-190.00 | 185.00-200.00 |
| Birdcage | 1939 | 150.00-175.00 | 125.00-150.00 | 150.00-175.00 |
| Doughnut | 1938 | 85.00-100.00 | **85.00-100.00 | 100.00-125.00 |
| Football | 1938 | 275.00-300.00 | 275.00-300.00 | 300.00-325.00 |

*canary 35.00-42.00
**ivory 50.00-55.00

**Row 1:** Automobile, cobalt; automobile, canary/gold; automobile, maroon/silver. **Row 2:** Basket, canary/silver; basketball, turquoise/gold; basketball, Chinese red. **Row 3:** Birdcage, maroon/silver; birdcage, cadet; doughnut, cobalt. **Row 4:** Doughnut, ivory; football, cobalt; football, cobalt/gold.

# Airflow, Aladdin, French Teapots

The Airflow teapot was introduced in 1940. It is commonly found in the six cup-size and less frequently in the eight cup-size. There are a wide variety of colors available. Some teapots are also gold decorated. The most common colors are turquoise, cobalt and canary.

The six cup Aladdin-shape teapot is very common and was used by Hall with a vast assortment of decals. Also, just about every solid color Aladdin seems to exist. The Aladdin teapot with the round lid was introduced in 1939. In 1940, an optional infusor was offered. A few years later Hall tried the Aladdin teapot with the oval lid and oval infusor. However, by the end of World War II the teapot with the round opening was reinstated. This limited production of the teapot with the oval opening has made it much harder to find than its sister with the round opening. Notice the marine teapot. It is part of the Gold Label line which is discussed on page 108.

French teapots are found in a wide range of colors and sizes. Sizes include 1,1½,2,3,4,6,8,10, and 12 cups. The most frequently found teapots are the six cup and eight cup sizes. Many of the French-style teapots will be found with gold decoration. The two teapots on the left on the bottom shelf are part of the Gold Label line (see page 108).

| Teapot | Solid Colors | Gold/Silver Decorated | Gold Label |
|---|---|---|---|
| Airflow, 6 cup | 18.00-22.00 | 27.00-35.00 | |
| Airflow, 8 cup | 22.00-27.00 | 30.00-40.00 | |
| Aladdin, oval opening | 18.00-20.00 | 20.00-25.00 | |
| Aladdin, round opening | 14.00-16.00 | 18.00-25.00 | 32.00-35.00 |
| French, 1-4 cup | 15.00-18.00 | 20.00-25.00 | 23.00-27.00 |
| French, 6-8 cup | 14.00-18.00 | 20.00-27.00 | 25.00-28.00 |
| French, 10-12 cup | 20.00-25.00 | 30.00-35.00 | |

**Row 1:** Airflow, 6 cup, maroon; Airflow, 6 cup, canary/gold; Airflow, 8 cup, turquoise/gold.
**Row 2:** Aladdin, oval lid, Monterrey/gold; Aladdin, oval lid, cadet/gold; Aladdin, oval lid/infusor, warm yellow/gold; Aladdin, oval lid, Chinese red. **Row 3:** Aladdin, round lid, canary/gold; Aladdin, round lid, camellia/gold; Aladdin, round lid, marine, Gold Label; Aladdin, round lid, black lustre/gold. **Row 4:** French, 6 cup, ivory, Gold Label; French, 4 cup, cadet, Gold Label; French, 3 cup, cobalt/gold; French, 2 cup, Stock Brown; French, 2 cup, canary.

# Globe, Hook Cover, Melody Teapots

The six cup Globe teapot is shown with both types of spouts. The turndown style is called dripless. Finding the Globe is difficult. Notice the different style of gold decoration of the Globe and the dripless Globe teapots. Also, the blue teapot on the top row is an unusual shade--close to but somewhat lighter than delphinium.

The Hook Cover teapot holds six cups. It was introduced in 1940 and the most common colors are cadet and delphinium. This teapot is very common and hard-to-sell even with gold decoration.

The six cup Melody teapot was first offered in 1939. This is a hard-to-find teapot and very desirable among collectors. The small two cup stock green teapot in the photograph is still in production.

| Teapot | Red/Cobalt | Other Colors | Gold/Silver Decorated | Gold Label |
|---|---|---|---|---|
| Globe | 60.00-65.00 | 40.00-45.00 | 70.00-75.00 | |
| Globe, dripless | 60.00-65.00 | 42.00-47.00 | 70.00-75.00 | |
| Hook Cover | 30.00-35.00 | 12.00-14.00 | 14.00-16.00 | 16.00-18.00 |
| Melody, 6 cup | 80.00-85.00 | 80.00-85.00 | | |

**Row 1:** Globe, Monterrey; Globe, medium blue; Globe, Monterrey/gold. **Row 2:** Globe, dripless spout, cobalt/gold; globe, dripless spout, rose/gold; Globe, dripless spout, Addison/gold. **Row 3:** Hook Cover, Chinese red; Hook Cover, cadet/gold; Hook Cover, maroon/gold. **Row 4:** Melody, canary/gold; Melody, Chinese red; Melody, Stock Green.

# Teapots

The Moderne style teapot is a six cup teapot found in a limited number of colors. The most common colors are ivory, canary, and cadet. Gold decoration is limited to the tip of the spout, the foot, and the knob of the lid. This teapot is very plain and even the gold decorated ones are not easy to sell.

The Nautilus is a sea shell-shaped six cup teapot which made its appearance in 1939. This teapot is hard-to-find and commands a good price. Gold decoration is only a few simple lines as may be seen on the turquoise teapot in the photo.

The Parade teapot is a common six cup teapot. It is easily found in canary. Other colors are more challenging to find.

The Rhythm teapot is very hard-to-find with a good lid. Due to the design of the teapot, not many lids survived. This is a six cup teapot and was introduced in 1939.

The "Sundial" teapot is found most often in canary. It is a six cup teapot which was part of the kitchenware line. The "Sundial" teapot also comes in 8 oz. and 10 oz. individual sizes. These sizes were still available recently at the "Hall Closet" in Stock Green and Stock Brown.

The Columbia is an interesting early teapot. This is the only one we have seen. It has a #2 mark on the bottom with the numbers 15-80 in place of "MADE IN USA."

"Pert" teapots are part of the kitchenware line. The "HALL'S SUPERIOR QUALITY KITCHENWARE" mark is found on the bottom of the red and white teapot. Colors other than the Chinese red with the Hi-white handle, or the decaled cadet of the Rose Parade line are not common. Both six cup and four cup sizes may be found.

| Teapot | Red/Cobalt | Other Colors | Gold/Silver Decorated | Gold Label |
|---|---|---|---|---|
| Moderne | | 12.00-14.00 | 14.00-16.00 | |
| Nautilus | 90.00-100.00 | 60.00-70.00 | 70.00-80.00 | |
| Parade | 45.00-55.00 | 12.00-14.00 | 14.00-16.00 | 18.00-20.00 |
| Rhythm | 85.00-95.00 | 45.00-50.00 | 50.00-60.00 | |
| Columbia | 135.00-145.00 | | | |
| "Sundial" | 55.00-60.00 | 40.00-45.00 | 50.00-55.00 | |
| "Pert", 4 cup | 16.00-18.00 | 14.00-16.00 | 22.00-25.00 | |
| "Pert", 6 cup | 22.00-25.00 | 18.00-20.00 | 25.00-27.00 | |

**Row 1:** Moderne, ivory/gold; Nautilus, Chinese red; Nautilus, turquoise/gold. **Row 2:** Parade, canary/gold; Rhythm, cobalt/gold; Rhythm, Monterrey/gold. **Row 3:** "Sundial", cobalt; "Sundial", canary/gold; "Sundial", Blue Blossom; "Sundial", marine. **Row 4:** Columbia, cobalt/gold; "Pert", red/white; "Pert", canary/gold.

# Star, Stramline, Surfside, Windshield Teapots

The Star teapot has been named for its style of decoration. This is a common six cup teapot introduced in 1940. The only colors we have seen are turquoise and cobalt. This same shape is also used with the World's Fair trylon and perisphere decoration (see page 139).

The six cup Streamline first appeared in 1937. Lids are easily damaged, so be careful. Streamlines are common in delphinium. They may be found with either gold or silver decoration.

The Surfside is a six cup teapot introduced in 1937. It is hard-to-find, but is most common in emerald green. Many people confuse this teapot and the Nautilus.

The Windshield, a six cup teapot, was first offered in 1941. There are a variety of colors available. Most of these teapots are gold decorated. Camellia is the most common color. The teapot with the vegetable decal is not easy to find and is very desirable. Another decal which may be found on this teapot pictures ducks and geese. These teapots with the decals bear the "HALLS SUPERIOR QUALITY KITCHENWARE" mark. The ivory teapot with the gold dots is part of the Gold Label line.

| Teapot | Red/Cobalt | Other Colors | Gold/Silver Decorated | Gold Label |
|--------|-----------|--------------|----------------------|------------|
| Star | 25.00-27.00 | | 20.00-22.00 | |
| Streamline | 35.00-40.00 | 16.00-18.00 | 18.00-22.00 | |
| Surfside | 75.00-85.00 | 55.00-60.00 | 65.00-70.00 | |
| *Windshield | 50.00-55.00 | 16.00-18.00 | 18.00-20.00 | 18.00-20.00 |
| *With decals | 40.00-45.00 | | | |

**Row 1:** Star, turquoise/gold; Star, cobalt/gold; Streamline, emerald. **Row 2:** Streamline, canary/gold; Streamline, delphinium; Streamline, Chinese red. **Row 3:** Surfside, maroon/gold; Surfside, emerald/gold; Windshield, ivory/dot, Gold Label. **Row 4:** Windshield, ivory, carrot and beet decal; Windshield, cobalt/gold; Windshield, camellia/gold.

# Albany, Baltimore, Boston, Cleveland, Hollywood Teapots

The Albany teapot is a six cup teapot which was introduced in the early thirties. It may be found in solid colors and with gold decoration. This style teapot was also included in the Gold Label line.

The Baltimore teapot is another teapot introduced in the early thirties. The most common colors are emerald and marine. Pictured is a teapot from the Gold Label line of the fifties. Another interesting Baltimore teapot with a decal is shown in the photograph on page 139.

Production of the Boston style teapot began very early and has continued to the present. Sizes made include 1,1½,2,3,4,6, and 8 cup. The cobalt teapot on the top shelf has the letters "HALL" embossed and a gold stamp stating "Clinton and Phillips Domestic Teapots."

The Cleveland is a six cup teapot which is not easily found. It is much more attractive with gold decoration than without.

The Hollywood teapot was introduced in the late twenties. It is found in three sizes--4,6, and 8 cup--and in a variety of colors. The Hollywood teapot was later used in the Gold Label line.

| Teapot | Red/Cobalt | Other Colors | Gold/Silver Decorated | Gold Label |
|---|---|---|---|---|
| Albany | 37.00-42.00 | 32.00-35.00 | 37.00-40.00 | 40.00-45.00 |
| Baltimore | 27.00-30.00 | 22.00-25.00 | 27.00-30.00 | 32.00-35.00 |
| Boston, 1,1½,2 cup | 42.00-45.00 | 20.00-22.00 | 22.00-25.00 | |
| Boston, 3,4 cup | 40.00-42.00 | 20.00-22.00 | 22.00-25.00 | |
| Boston, 6 cup | 35.00-40.00 | 18.00-20.00 | 20.00-25.00 | 30.00-32.00 |
| Boston, 8 cup | 40.00-45.00 | 22.00-27.00 | 27.00-30.00 | |
| Cleveland | 32.00-37.00 | 30.00-32.00 | 32.00-35.00 | |
| Hollywood, 4,8 cup | 30.00-35.00 | 27.00-30.00 | 30.00-35.00 | |
| Hollywood, 6 cup | 30.00-35.00 | 16.00-18.00 | 20.00-22.00 | 25.00-27.00 |

**Row 1:** Albany, cobalt/gold; Baltimore, maroon, Gold Label; Boston, 6 cup, cobalt/gold.
**Row 2:** Boston, 8 cup, cadet/gold; Boston, 6 cup, maroon; Boston, 4 cup, canary/gold;
Boston, 2 cup, cobalt/gold. **Row 3:** Cleveland, turquoise; Cleveland, warm yellow/gold;
Cleveland, emerald/gold. **Row 4:** Hollywood, 8 cup, cobalt/gold; Hollywood, 8 cup,
delphinium/gold; Hollywood, 6 cup, Monterrey/gold; Hollywood, 6 cup, cadet/gold.

# Illinois, Los Angeles, Manhattan, Newport, New York, Philadephia Teapots

The Illinois teapot is very difficult to find. This was a very early teapot and was only produced for a few years. The most common color is cobalt. The Los Angeles teapot was introduced in the mid-twenties. It can be found in a number of colors and was made in the 4, 6, and 8 cup sizes. An example of the Gold Label design is shown in the picture.

The Manhattan teapot is shown complete with the dripper and spreader. In this form it is referred to as a "French drip coffee biggin." We have never seen this teapot with gold decoration.

The Newport style teapot was introduced in the early thirties. It is most commonly associated with the Autumn Leaf design but may also be found in solid colors. The Newport may be found with gold decoration or with a black decal.

The New York teapot was a very popular teapot which was added to the Gold Decorated line from the institutional line in 1920. There are many colors and the following sizes are available: 1, 1½, 2, 3, 4, 6, 8, and 12 cup. The four cup cobalt teapot in the picture is an example of a very early teapot. There are only a few simple gold lines for the decoration.

The Philadelphia teapot was included in the Gold Decorated line in 1923. Available sizes are 1½, 3, 4, 6, 8, and 10 cups. This teapot was used with a number of decorations. The pink teapot is an example of the Gold Label design. A hearth type decal is pictured on the Dresden color teapot. The gold decoration on the turquoise teapot is unusual.

| Teapot | Red/Cobalt | Other Colors | Gold/Silver Decorated | Gold Label |
|---|---|---|---|---|
| Illinois | 65.00-70.00 | 65.00-70.00 | 70.00-75.00 | |
| Los Angeles, 4, 8 cup | 30.00-35.00 | 22.00-27.00 | 27.00-30.00 | |
| Los Angeles, 6 cup | 28.00-32.00 | 18.00-20.00 | 22.00-25.00 | 25.00-28.00 |
| Manhattan | 22.00-25.00 | | | |
| Manhattan, with dripper | | 32.00-35.00 | | |
| Newport | | 18.00-20.00 | 50.00-55.00 | |
| New York, 1, 1½, 2 cup | 25.00-27.00 | 18.00-20.00 | 20.00-22.00 | |
| New York, 3 4 cup | 25.00-27.00 | 16.00-18.00 | 18.00-20.00 | |
| New York, 6 cup | 25.00-27.00 | 14.00-16.00 | 16.00-18.00 | 22.00-25.00 |
| New York, 8 12 cup | 30.00-32.00 | 18.00-20.00 | 25.00-27.00 | |

| Teapot | Red/Cobalt | Other Colors | Gold/Silver Decorated | Gold Label |
|---|---|---|---|---|
| Philadelphia, 1½ cup | | | 45.00-50.00 | |
| Philadelphia, 3, 4 cup | | 20.00-22.00 | 25.00-27.00 | |
| Philadelphia, 6 cup | 27.00-30.00 | 16.00-18.00 | 22.00-25.00 | 18.00-20.00 |
| Philadelphia, 8, 10 cup | | 22.00-25.00 | 30.00-32.00 | |

**Row 1:** Illinois, cobalt/gold; Los Angeles, Monterrey, Gold Label; Los Angeles, maroon.
**Row 2:** Manhattan ("French drip coffee biggin"), mahogany; Manhattan ("French drip coffee biggin"), maroon; Newport, pink. **Row 3:** New York, 6 cup, cobalt/gold; New York, 4 cup, cobalt/gold; New York, 2 cup, pink; New York, 2 cup, ivory/gold. **Row 4:** Philadelphia, pink, Gold Label; Philadelphia, cobalt/gold; Philadelphia, marine; Philadelphia, Stock Brown.

# Coverlet, McCormick, Teamaster, Cube Teapots

The "Coverlet" teapot has a metal cover with cut-outs for the spout and handle. The teapot in the center has the metal cover removed to show the shape of the teapot. These teapots are marked "Made exclusively for the FORMAN FAMILY, INC. by THE HALL CHINA CO., U.S.A." The teapot may be found in various colors and came with both silver and gold color covers.

The McCormick teapot was made as a premium item for the McCormick Tea Company. The teapots are marked "McCORMICK, BALTIMORE, MARYLAND." Stock brown, turquoise, and maroon are the most common colors.

The Teataster was an oval, 2-compartment teapot made for the Teamaster Company in the forties. Most of the teapots are plain, but a few have been found with gold decoration. The mark on the bottom will usually state "TEAMASTER, MADE BY HALL IN U.S.A."

Twinspouts are round 2-compartment teapots made for the Teamaster Company. The teapots are usually marked "TWINSPOUT, TEAMASTER, Pat. No. 2135410." Some of the teapots produced later may be marked "INVENTO PRODUCTS."

The diamond-shape Twinspouts were also made for the Teamaster Company. These are 2-compartment teapots and have the same mark on the bottom as the Twinspouts above.

The Cubes are two cup teapots made by Hall and several other companies under a British patent. The Hall teapots will have the Hall #3 mark, the patent numbers, and the following inscription on the bottom: "CUBE TEAPOTS, LIMITED, LEICESTER."

| Teapot | Red/Cobalt | Other Colors | Gold/Silver Decorated |
|---|---|---|---|
| "Coverlet" | | 18.00-20.00 | |
| McCormick | | 18.00-20.00 | 27.00-32.00 |
| Teataster | 70.00-75.00 | 50.00-55.00 | 57.00-62.00 |
| Twinspout, round | 45.00-50.00 | 40.00-45.00 | 45.00-50.00 |
| Twinspout, diamond | 47.00-52.00 | 40.00-45.00 | |
| Cube | 37.00-40.00 | 30.00-35.00 | |

**Row 1:** "Coverlet", canary; "Coverlet", pink; "Coverlet", ivory. **Row 2:** McCormick, turquoise; McCormick, maroon; McCormick, cadet. **Row 3:** Teataster, turquoise; Twinspout, emerald; Twinspout, warm yellow; Twinspout, canary/gold. **Row 4:** Twinspout, Chinese red; Twinspout, turquoise; Twinspout, maroon; Cube, emerald; Cube, black.

# Twin-Tee, Tea for Two, Morning Teapots

Twin-Tee sets were introduced in 1926. They consist of two pots and a tray upon which the pots set. There is a short spout pot which is used for hot water and a long spout pot which is used for the tea. Twin-Tee sets come in a wide variety of colors. There are also several styles of floral decals and a few different gold decorations. The warm yellow teapot in the photo is marked "BLUE BELL TEAPOT NO.1"

The Tea for Two sets differ from the above Twin-Tee sets in several ways. The tops of the Tea for Two teapots are angled rather than flat. The trays of the Tea for Two sets do not have the full-length center division like the Twin-Tee trays. Tea for Two sets have much simpler gold decorations and don't appear to have the elaborate floral decals. There is also a larger version of this style teapot called Tea for Four.

The yellow teapot on the third shelf is not Hall, but is a good copy of the round T-Ball shown on page 139. Notice the handle of this teapot is smooth and Boston-like. The Hall T-Ball has a small raised thumb grip on a New York-style handle.

The small Morning teapots are not easily found. They were made as sets with matching sugars and creamers. A matching set is shown in the photograph on the next page. Morning teapots are found in various solid colors and in several of the decal lines. Matching cups and saucers have been found for one set. However, if cups and saucers were made to go with all the color sets, we have not seen them. See Blue Blossom and Blue Garden for additional sets.

| Teapot | Red/Cobalt | Other Colors | Decorated |
|---|---|---|---|
| Twin-Tee set | 45.00-50.00 | 32.00-37.00 | 45.00-50.00 |
| Tea for Two set | 45.00-50.00 | 30.00-32.00 | 35.00-37.00 |
| Tea for Four set | 55.00-60.00 | 42.00-45.00 | 45.00-50.00 |
| Morning teapot | 35.00-40.00 | 28.00-32.00 | 45.00-50.00 |
| Morning sugar and creamer | 18.00-20.00 | 12.00-14.00 | 20.00-25.00 |

**Row 1:** Twin-Tee, black garden; Twin-Tee, Pansy; Twin-Tee, rose. **Row 2:** Twin-Tee, green/gold; Twin-Tee, cobalt; Twin-Tee, daffodil/black. **Row 3:** Tea-for-Two, pink/platinum; Twin Pouch, (not Hall); Morning teapot, backstamped "SET NO. 1 BLUE BELL". **Row 4:** Morning teapot; Boston, 2 cup, silver; "Cupid", 2 cup.

# Miscellaneous Teapots

This Chinese red Morning set is a nice addition to any collection. Morning sets are discussed on page 136. The Chicago style teapot has been in the institutional line for a long time and is still being offered today in four sizes.

The "Windcrest" is one of a series of teapots designed by J. Palin Thorley during the forties. This teapot has only been found in canary. Other teapots by this same designer will be found in the next few photographs.

The "Birch" is a Victorian-style teapot produced during the forties. It is found in blue turquoise and is not common with gold decoration.

The McCormick teapot in Stock Brown with this gold decoration is unusual. This is probably a very early teapot. It has the following backstamp: "McCORMICK CO. BANQUET TEAS--BALTO." The two cup McCormick with the embossing on the side is not a real old teapot. It will also be found in other colors.

The round T-Ball was introduced in 1948. It was made for Bacharach of New York and bears the mark "T-BALL TEAPOT--MADE FOR BACHARACH BY HALL CHINA COMPANY."

The World's Fair teapot incorporates the perisphere and trylon on a cobalt body with the star shape. It was made for the New York World's Fair in 1940. The teapot has the following backstamp: "A GENUINE HALL TEAPOT--MADE IN U.S.A.--SOLD EXCLUSIVELY AT THE NEW YORK WORLD'S FAIR--1940."

The "Tip-Pot" has two spouts but only one internal chamber. It sits in a metal holder with a candle warmer base. The teapot has the backstamp "TIP-POT--The ultimate in serving hot tea or coffee. 10 cup--FIREPROOF--HALL CHINA--ANOTHER FORMAN FAMILY U.S.A.PRODUCT."

The Mount Vernon and Cameo Rose teapots were part of larger dinnerware lines. Mount Vernon was made for Sears and Cameo Rose was made for the Jewel Company.

| Teapot | Solid Color | Decorated |
|---|---|---|
| "Coverlet", 2 cup | 12.00-14.00 | |
| Windcrest | 14.00-16.00 | 20.00-22.00 |
| "Birch" | 18.00-20.00 | 30.00-32.00 |
| McCormick | 18.00-20.00 | 27.00-32.00 |
| McCormick, 2 cup | 12.00-14.00 | |
| T-Ball, round | 32.00-37.00 | |
| World's Fair | | 150.00-175.00 |
| Tip-Pot | 50.00-55.00 | 60.00-65.00 |
| Mount Vernon | | 28.00-30.00 |
| Cameo Rose | | 32.00-37.00 |

**Row 1:** Morning teapot, Chinese red; Morning creamer and sugar, Chinese red; "Coverlet", 2 cup, cadet. **Row 2:** Windcrest, canary; Birch, blue turquoise; McCormick, brown/gold; McCormick, turquoise. **Row 3:** T-Ball, round, silver; World's Fair, cobalt; Baltimore, warm yellow. **Row 4:** "Tip-Pot", Hi-white; Mount Vernon; Cameo Rose.

# Victorian Style Teapots

The Victorian style teapots were introduced in the early forties. There are six teapots in this group. They have been given the following names: "Benjamin", "Murphy", "Plume", "Bowknot", "Birch" and "Connie". The first teapots were plain but gold decoration was added a few years later. This line was dropped by the end of the decade. We have never seen a gold decorated "Bejamin" or "Murphy".

The pink Grape teapot with the gold decoration is from the line designed by Thorley. It may also be found with jewel encrusted grapes or with a decal as seen on page 143. The pink color shown here is unusual for this style teapot.

The white teapot with the decal is from the Hallcraft line designed by Eva Zeisel. These pieces were available in the fifties in several patterns.

The Tritone teapot is from a kitchenware line which Hall produced during the fifties. Other pieces in this line may be found. See page 151 for the water bottle.

The Lipton teapot is the same as the six cup French-style teapot. It is distinguished by the "LIPTON TEA" stamp on the bottom. The most common colors are maroon and warm yellow.

| Teapot | Solid Color | Gold Decorated |
|--------|-------------|----------------|
| "Benjamin" | 20.00-22.00 | |
| "Murphy" | 22.00-25.00 | |
| "Plume" | 16.00-18.00 | 22.00-25.00 |
| "Bowknot" | 25.00-27.00 | 30.00-32.00 |
| "Birch" | 18.00-20.00 | 30.00-32.00 |
| "Connie" | 18.00-20.00 | 25.00-27.00 |
| Grape | 32.00-35.00 | 35.00-40.00 |
| Hallcraft | 14.00-17.00 | |
| Tritone | 40.00-45.00 | |
| Lipton | 12.00-14.00 | |

**Row 1:** "Plume", pink; "Bowknot", pink; "Benjamin", celadon. **Row 2:** "Connie", celadon; "Birch", turquoise blue; Grape, pink. **Row 3:** Windcrest, canary; "Murphy", turquoise blue; Hallcraft teapot. **Row 4:** Tri-tone teapot; Lipton, maroon; French, Chinese red/Hi-white.

# More Teapots

These Grape style teapots have some ornate decorations. The first has a Zeisel style decal and the second has rhinestones embedded in the grapes. Neither teapot is easy to find.

The side-handle Manhattan teapot is an early pot which we have never seen with gold decoration. It comes in a variety of colors and is still being sought after by quite a few collectors.

The Starlight teapot has a band of stars near the top. Some of these teapots will have rhinestones in these stars. The Royal teapot pictured is the only one we have seen. It can probably also be found without gold decoration.

The square T-Ball is a sister to the round T-Ball shown on page 139. It was also made for Bacharach, Inc. of New York. It is found in a number of colors, but we have not seen this teapot gold decorated.

The Bowling Ball is an odd-shaped teapot which dates to the late thirties. So far, we have seen it only in turquoise and cobalt. The Bowling Ball and the Kansas teapots are both very hard-to-find.

Ronald Reagan is a new but interesting teapot. Although it may still occasionally be found in the "Hall Closet" it doesn't gather dust on the shelves for very long. Maybe someone is speculating???

| Teapot | Solid Color | Decorated |
|---|---|---|
| Grape | 32.00-35.00 | 35.00-40.00 |
| Manhattan, side handle | 28.00-32.00 | |
| Starlight | 35.00-37.00 | 38.00-42.00 |
| Royal | 32.00-35.00 | 35.00-40.00 |
| T-Ball, Square | 32.00-37.00 | |
| Bowling Ball | 200.00-250.00 | |
| Kansas | 85.00-95.00 | 95.00-100.00 |
| Ronald Reagan | 27.00-30.00 | |

**Row 1:** Grape, with decal; Grape, with jewels; Manhattan, side-handle, maroon; Manhattan, side-handle, cobalt. **Row 2:** Starlight, canary; Royal, white/gold; T-Ball square, ivory. **Row 3:** Bowling ball, turquoise; Indiana, warm yellow; Ronald Reagan.

The pink teapot with the gold dots is the Ohio. The maroon teapot is a Thorley design we are calling "Regal." This is the only one we have seen, but it also probably comes with gold trim. The small black teapot was an exclusive design for the Iron Gate Products Co. Inc. of New York. We have only seen it in this black color. The green teapot does not have a "Hall" mark, but is similar in shape to another teapot which has been found recently with a "Hall" mark. The quality of this teapot approaches those made by Hall. Maybe someone will eventually find this teapot with an identifying mark.

| Teapot | Solid Color | Gold Decorated |
|---|---|---|
| Ohio | | 55.00-65.00 |
| Regal | 37.00-40.00 | 42.00-45.00 |
| Iron Gate | | 16.00-18.00 |

This interesting Hall teapot has just been discovered. It remains to be seen how many will eventually be found, but there are great odds against any significant quantity ever showing up. A find such as this keeps collectors interested in searching for more unusual pieces of Hall china.

145

# Drip Coffee Pots

The coffee pot with the metal base has a design which has been seen on a few other Hall pieces. We have not found the name of the design and none of the pieces are easily found.

The all-china coffee pots need four pieces to be complete. They consist of the base, the dripper, the lid and a china spreader which fits inside the dripper. The "Lorraine" drip coffee pot is most commonly associated with the Autumn Leaf line.

The "Rounded Terrace" coffee pot comes in several decal patterns and in two sizes. The "Imperial" and "Princess" coffee pots were produced for the Tricolator Company. They have metal drippers and may be used with or without the metal dripper, since a china lid was also included.

| Coffee Pot | Price |
|---|---|
| Coffee pot, metal base | 55.00-60.00 |
| "Lorraine" drip, cadet/white | 42.00-45.00 |
| Coffee pot, Shaggy Tulip | 60.00-65.00 |
| Coffee pot, "Medallion" | 45.00-50.00 |
| Coffee pot, #691 | 45.00-55.00 |
| "Rounded Terrace", small-size | 22.00-25.00 |
| "Rounded Terrace", large-size | 25.00-27.00 |
| Imperial | 35.00-39.00 |
| Princess | 37.00-40.00 |

**Row 1:** Drip coffee, metal base; Drip coffee, "Lorraine", cadet/white; Drip-O-lator, Shaggy tulip. **Row 2:** Drip coffee, "Medallion", lettuce; #691 drip coffee, Chinese red; #691 drip coffee, black/white. **Row 3:** "Rounded Terrace" Drip-O-lator; Drip coffee, "Imperial", lettuce; Drip coffee, "Princess".

# Drip-O-lators and Other Coffee Pots

Drip-O-lator was a extensive line of coffee pots made for the Enterprise Aluminum Company from the thirties until the seventies. Enterprise Aluminum supplied the metal dripper and marketed the coffee pots under the Drip-O-lator label. There are many shapes of Drip-O-lator pots which are not pictured here. Some of these other pots were made by Hall and some were made by other china companies. They will all have the Drip-O-lator mark. Most of the coffee pots made by other china companies will also bear their backstamp in addition to the Drip-O-lator mark. The ones made by Hall do not have a "HALL" mark.

Two other Drip-O-lator coffee pots, the "Target" and the "Jerry" are shown on the next page.

| Coffee Pot | *Price |
|---|---|
| "Viking", Drip-O-lator | 28.00-30.00 |
| "Target", Drip-O-lator | 30.00-32.00 |
| "Waverly", Drip-O-lator | 18.00-20.00 |
| "Cloverleaf", Drip-O-lator | 35.00-37.00 |
| Drape, Drip-O-lator | 25.00-27.00 |
| "Jerry", Drip-O-lator | 35.00-37.00 |
| Cathedral, Drip-Oplator | 18.00-20.00 |
| "Dart" | 18.00-20.00 |
| Coffee pot, Duchess | 22.00-25.00 |
| Coffee pot, Baron | 32.00-35.00 |

*Includes metal dripper

**Row 1:** "Waverly", small-size; "Waverly", large-size; "Cathedral", large-size. **Row 2:** "Viking", Cactus decal; "Viking", Bird of Paradise decal; "Viking, Flamingo decal. **Row 3:** Drip coffee, "Drape"; Drip coffe, cloverleaf style; Drip coffee, "Dart". **Row 4:** "Duchess", Chinese red; "Baron", Chinese red.

# Electric Percolators and Later Hall Products

These electric percolators have Westinghouse heating elements. They can be found in plain solid colors and with decals. The percolator with the RX decal came with matching dinnerware and kitchenware items. We bought a set a long time ago. It was supposed to have been a premium item for some pharmaceutical company.

The pieces on the bottom shelf were made during the fifties and later. The coffee pot is part of the Hallcraft line which came in eight different patterns--Caprice, Dawn, Arizona, Fantasy, Holiday, Harlequin, Peach Blossom, and Buckingham. These patterns are slowly beginning to make their appearance at the flea markets.

The Flareware kitchen line has not attracted very much collector interest. Other pieces besides the cookie jar include a casserole, a teapot, a coffee server with warmer, a salad bowl, and a 3-piece bowl set.

| Item | Price |
|---|---|
| Percolator, solid color | 30.00-32.00 |
| Percolator, decal | 50.00-60.00 |
| "Jerry", Drip-O-lator | 35.00-37.00 |
| "Target", Drip-O-lator | 30.00-32.00 |
| Coffee pot, Hallcraft | 18.00-20.00 |
| Water bottle, Tritone | 45.00-50.00 |
| Casserole, Flareware | 8.00-10.00 |
| Cookie jar, Flareware | 8.00-10.00 |
| Coffee server and warmer, Flareware | 27.00-30.00 |
| Salad bowl, Flareware | 4.00-6.00 |
| Teapot, Flareware | 18.00-20.00 |
| Bowl set, 3-pc., Flareware | 10.00-14.00 |

**Row 1:** Electric percolator, geese decal; electric percolator, pink; electric percolator, pheasant decal. **Row 2:** Drip-O-lator, "Jerry"; electric percolator, RX decal; Drip-O-lator, "Target". **Row 3:** Coffee pot, Hallcraft; water bottle, Tritone; cookie jar, Flare Ware

Left: Forman Brothers electric warmer; Right: Art Deco casserole in metal holder.

# Westinghouse and the Forman Family

The electric coffee makers came with matching sugars and creamers. The heating elements were made by Westinghouse. There are a great number of these style coffee makers, but very few of the patterns can be attributed to Hall. The problem of identification is complicated, since there is usually no mark on the coffee maker except for the manufacturer of the heating element.

The Forman Family bought pieces from Hall and other potteries to be used in the manufacture of their products. Examples of these items are shown on this page and by the Fuji pattern waffle iron. Many other pieces like these were made, but it is usually not possible to determine who supplied the china parts.

| Item | Price |
|---|---|
| Coffeemaker, Cattail (2 styles) | 75.00-85.00 |
| Sugar and creamer, Cattail | 30.00-35.00 |
| Heating element, Cattail | 45.00-50.00 |
| Coffeemaker, Hanging vine (2 styles) | 50.00-60.00 |
| Sugar and creamer, Hanging vine | 20.00-25.00 |
| Waffle iron, Fuji | 22.00-25.00 |
| Sugar and creamer, Fuji | 18.00-20.00 |
| Casserole, Art Deco in holder | 25.00-27.00 |
| Warmer, Forman Bros. | 37.00-40.00 |

**Row 1:** Coffeemaker, electric, Hanging vine; sugar, Hanging vine; coffeemaker, electric, Hanging vine. **Row 2:** Coffeemaker, electric, Cattail; Creamer and sugar, Cattail; coffeemaker, electric, Cattail. **Row 3:** Sugar and creamer, Cattail; heating element, Cattail; sugar, Fuji; waffle iron, Fuji.

# Part V: Other Hall Products

Beer sets came in solid colors and with decals. There was a large tankard pitcher with two different style mugs. The flagon style mug is shown here and the barrel type mug is pictured on page 157. The flagon came in five sizes and the barrel shape was available in two sizes. There are several decal scenes, two of which are shown in the picture. There was also a matching pretzel jar available with the decals.

|  | **Solid Colors** | **Decals** |
|---|---|---|
| Tankard pitcher | 32.00-35.00 | 85.00-95.00 |
| Flagon, 8,10,12,14,16 oz. | 8.00-9.00 | 30.00-35.00 |
| Barrel mug, 8, 12 oz. | 7.00-9.00 | |
| Pretzel jar | | 75.00-85.00 |

The Old Crow Punch set consists of 12 cups, a ladle and the punch bowl. It is an interesting set, but is not very old. Quite a few sets have been turning up in the original boxes.

| Set in box | 125.00-150.00 |
|---|---|

Tom and Jerry sets were introduced in the thirties. They were made in ivory and Hi-black colors. The covered sets held five quarts and were sold with the #2044 mug.

| | |
|---|---:|
| Covered Tom and Jerry bowl | 28.00-30.00 |
| Tom and Jerry #2044 mug | 2.00-2.25 |

The Tom and Jerry bowl on the right is a footed four quart bowl and was sold with a five ounce mug. The Tom and Jerry Plum Pudding bowl on the left holds eight quarts and came with a seven ounce mug.

| | |
|---|---:|
| Tom and Jerry bowl, footed | 18.00-20.00 |
| Tom and Jerry Plum Pudding bowl | 22.00-25.00 |
| Tom and Jerry mug, 5 oz. | 1.75-2.00 |
| Tom and Jerry mug, 7 oz. | 2.00-2.25 |

# Vases, Mugs, and Advertising Items

Hall produced a variety of items for hotels and restaurants. Some of those items are shown here.

|  | Price |
|---|---|
| Row 1: 1. This is not a Hall piece. | |
| 2. Trumpet vase, maroon | 6.00-8.00 |
| 3. Trumpet vase, cobalt | 7.00-9.00 |
| 4. Vase, daffodil | 4.00-5.00 |
| | |
| Row 2: 1. Turkish coffee cup, #1270 | 4.00-5.00 |
| 2. Barrel mug, 8 oz. | 5.00-6.00 |
| 3. Mug, footed, #2274 | 4.00-5.00 |
| 4. Braniff International mug | 4.50-5.50 |
| 5. Cylindrical mug, #1314 | 4.00-5.00 |
| | |
| Row 3: 1. Ashtray, Palmer House | 7.00-9.00 |
| 2. Ashtray | 6.00-8.00 |
| 3. Ashtray | 7.00-9.00 |
| 4. Ashtray | 6.00-8.00 |
| 5. Ashtray with matchholder | 5.00-7.00 |
| | |
| Row 4: 1. Ashtray | 6.00-7.00 |
| 2. Ashtray | 4.00-5.00 |
| 3. Ashtray | 6.00-8.00 |
| 4. Ashtray, #696 | 3.00-4.00 |
| | |
| Row 5: 1. Butter pat, Regency Hotel | 2.50-3.50 |
| 2. Ashtray, #679 | 3.00-4.00 |
| 3. United Airlines bowl | 7.00-9.00 |
| 4. Spittoon | 18.00-20.00 |

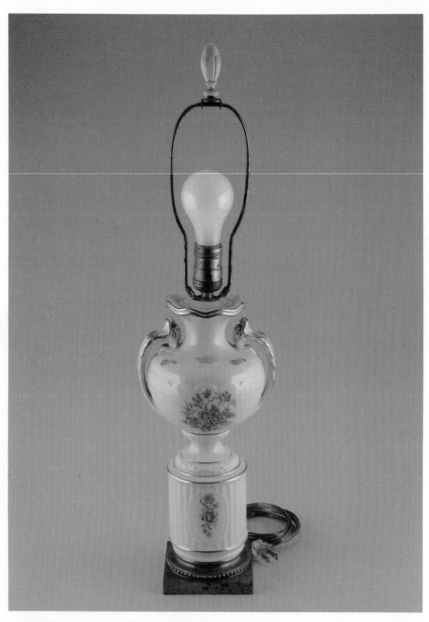

Several lamps are known to have been made by Hall. However, since these lamps were not marked with the "Hall" stamp, it is hard to identify Hall lamps today. If you look closely, you will see an original Hall paper label on the lamp in the picture. It has the shape of an Aladdin teapot.

Hall table lamp                                              30.00-35.00

# OTHER BOOKS ON CHINA, POTTERY AND DINNERWARE

| | |
|---|---|
| The Collector's Encyclopedia of Depression Glass, 6th Edition—Florence | $17.95 |
| Pocket Guide to Depression Glass, 4th Edition—Florence | $9.95 |
| Blue Ridge Dinnerware, 2nd Edition—Newbound | $9.95 |
| Blue Willow—Gaston | $9.95 |
| Children's Dishes—Whitmyer | $9.95 |
| Children's Glass Dishes, China, Furniture—Lechler | $17.95 |
| The Collector's Encyclopedia of American Dinnerware—Cunningham | $24.95 |
| The Collector's Encyclopedia of Flow Blue China—Gaston | $19.95 |
| The Collector's Encyclopedia of Akro Agate—Florence | $9.95 |
| The Collector's Encyclopedia of Fiesta—Huxford | $9.95 |
| The Collector's Encyclopedia of McCoy Pottery—Huxford | $19.95 |
| The Collector's Encyclopedia of Roseville, | $19.95 |
| The Collector's Encyclopedia of Roseville Pottery 2nd Series—Huxford | $19.95 |
| Elegant Glassware of the Depression Era—Florence | $17.95 |
| Franciscan Ware—Enge | $9.95 |
| Kitchen Glassware of The Depression Years—Florence | $19.95 |
| Shawnee Pottery—Simon | $8.95 |
| Versatile Vernon Kilns, Book II—Nelson | $9.95 |

Ask for these popular books at your favorite bookstore or order direct.

(Please add $1.00 postage and handling)

**Collector Books ● P.O. Box 3009 ● Paducah, Kentucky 42001**

# Two Important Tools For The
# Astute Antique Dealer, Collector and Investor

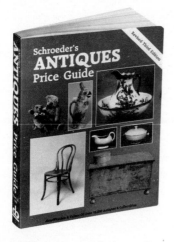

## Schroeder's Antiques Price Guide

The very best low cost investment that you can make if you are really serious about antiques and collectibles is a good identification and price guide. We publish and highly recommend **Schroeder's Antiques Price Guide.** Our editors and writers are very careful to seek out and report accurate values each year. We do not simply change the values of the items each year but start anew to bring you an entirely new edition. If there are repeats, they are by chance and not by choice. Each huge edition (it weighs 3 pounds!) has over 56,000 descriptions and current values on 608 - 8½x11 pages. There are hundreds and hundreds of categories and even more illustrations. Each topic is introduced by an interesting discussion that is an education in itself. Again, no dealer, collector or investor can afford not to own this book. It is available from your favorite bookseller or antiques dealer at the low price of $9.95. If you are unable to find this price guide in your area, it's available from Collector Books, P. O. Box 3009, Paducah, KY 42001 at $9.95 plus $1.00 for postage and handling.

## Schroeder's INSIDER and Price Update

**A monthly newsletter published for the antiques and collectibles marketplace.**

The **"INSIDER"**, as our subscribers have fondly dubbed it, is a monthly newsletter published for the antiques and collectibles marketplace. It gives the readers timely information as to trends, price changes, new finds, and market moves both upward and downward. Our writers are made up of a panel of well-known experts in the fields of Glass, Pottery, Dolls, Furniture, Jewelry, Country, Primitives, Oriental and a host of other fields in our huge industry. Our subscribers have that "inside edge" that makes them more profitable. Each month we explore 8-10 subjects that are "in", and close each discussion with a random sampling of current values that are recorded at press

time. Thousands of subscribers eagerly await each monthly issue of this timely 16-page newsletter. A sample copy is available for $3.00 postpaid. Subscriptions are postpaid at $24.00 for 12-months; 24 months for $45.00; 36 months for $65.00. A sturdy 3-ring binder to store your **Insider** is available for $5.00 postpaid. This newsletter contains NO paid advertising and is not available on your newsstand. It may be ordered by sending your check or money order to Collector Books, P. O. Box 3009, Paducah, KY 42001.